# Multinational Enterprises and Technological Spillovers

**Studies in Global Competition**
*Edited by John Cantwell, The University of Reading, UK and David Mowery, University of California, Berkeley, USA*

This book is part of a series. The publisher will accept continuation orders which may be cancelled at any time and which provide for automatic billing and shipping of each title in the series upon publication. Please write for details.

# Multinational Enterprises and Technological Spillovers

*Tommaso Perez*
*Ufficio Italiano Dei Cambi*
*Rome, Italy*

 **harwood academic publishers**
Australia • Canada • China • France • Germany • India • Japan • Luxembourg
Malaysia • The Netherlands • Russia • Singapore • Switzerland • Thailand

Amsteldijk 166
1st Floor
1079 LH Amsterdam
The Netherlands

---

**British Library Cataloguing in Publication Data**

Perez, Tommaso
   Multinational enterprises and technological spillovers
   1. International business enterprises   2. Technology transfer
   I. Title
   338.8'83

   ISBN 90-5702-295-8
   ISSN 1023-6147

*To Giusy and to my parents*

# Table of Contents

# List of Figures

# List of Tables

# Acknowledgements

This book is based on the previous work I did at the University of Ancona for my Doctoral thesis. Before and after I finished my thesis I benefited from the help of many scholars and friends who assisted me in a number of ways.

First of all I wish to thank the team of my supervisors, Pier Carlo Padoan (University of Rome) and Alessandro Sterlacchini (University of Ancona) who followed the development of this research throughout all its steps. Giuliano Conti and Valeriano Balloni, both at the University of Ancona, also gave me precious suggestions. Discussions with the members of the Faculty of the *Doctoral Tutorial* organised in occasion of the *1995 Annual Conference of the European International Business Academy* (Yair Aharoni, Peter Buckley, Danny Van Den Bulcke, John Dunning, Jean François Hennart and Stephen Young) and with the other participants in the conference (in particular, John Cantwell, Rajneesh Narula and Roberto Schiattarella) were also very valuable indeed and gave me a precious encouragement to going on with my research. Adrian Belton, Claudio Casadio, Aldo Femia, Paolo Ramazzotti, Francesca Sanna Randaccio were also among the people that helped me in this work. I also gratefully acknowledge Marco Ceccagnoli, Sergio Mariotti and Marco Mutinelli for providing me with a large part of the data which I used in this book.

Any opinions expressed in this book are those of the author and do not reflect those of Ufficio Italiano Dei Cambi.

# 1. Introduction

## 1.1. INTRODUCTION

The topics discussed in this book form part of wide-ranging debate on the consequences of the *internationalisation* or *globalisation* of the world economy. Whereas until only a few decades ago it seemed reasonable to concentrate analysis on the effects of the internationalisation of production on the developing countries, today it is the more developed economies that must confront the challenges raised by the growing openness of national economic systems.

Since the end of the 1970s, the concentration of foreign direct investment (FDI) internally to the countries that make up the Triad (United States, Europe, Japan), as well as the growing number of international agreements for cooperation among firms from those countries, have made their economies the most susceptible to the consequences of the international mobility of the production factors, of goods, and of technological knowledge. It is this that justifies the close attention paid by economists to these phenomena. On the one hand, given the pronounced mobility of production capital, the danger arises that erroneous economic and industrial policy choices may hamper the development of the national economies and favour those other countries which are better able to exploit the opportunities afforded by the globalisation of national productive and innovative systems. On the other hand, the question arises as to whether the internationalisation of the economy may not reduce the capacity of governments to control and direct national economies, with

1

dramatic effects on the dynamics of the fundamental economic magnitudes, primarily employment.

A set of factors further heighten alarm on both sides of the Atlantic. Not least of them is the ability of Japanese firms to impose their innovative products on world markets and to circumvent customs barriers. This combines with the economic take-off achieved by certain countries of South-East Asia, which have made the internationalisation of their economies the driving force of the development of their productive and technological bases.

The economic systems of the Western countries have responded differently to the challenges raised by the globalisation of the economy, and often in direct competition with each other. Thus, even internally to areas of close social, economic and political integration like the European Union, one discerns highly diverse, if not divergent, national policies pursued *vis-à-vis* the problems raised by the internationalisation of the economy. For example, since the early 1980s Great Britain has accelerated the internationalisation of its industrial structure by cautiously combining *laissez-faire* policies with measures designed to promote FDI in the country. Other countries, France for example, have maintained industrial policies designed to favour domestic industries and to orient the activity of foreign multinational enterprises (MNEs) on their territory. Yet others, Italy for instance, have taken no action at all, leaving it to national and foreign entrepreneurial forces to involve their national productive and innovative systems in the processes of economic internationalisation.

Leaving the political consequences of this state of affairs aside for the moment, investigation should be made of the internationalisation of economic systems in order to indicate possible strategies of action to national governments. The first step is to distinguish between two phenomena: *active internationalisation*, i.e. the foreign expansion of resident firms, and *passive internationalisation*, i.e. the involvement of foreign firms in a country's economic system. As discussed in the conclusions to this book, these two phenomena are closely interrelated, and they follow the same logic: the establishment of increasingly closer links among the productive and innovative systems of different countries. However, like the majority of studies on this topic, for ease of analysis this book tends to focus on only one of the two aspects of the problem: the process of passive internationalisation of national economic systems. Furthermore, given that the MNEs perform the predominant role in this process, the analysis conducted in the chapters that follow will focus on the effects of their actions on national productive and innovative systems.

Economic analysis was long divided between two antithetical views concerning the consequences of FDI on industry in countries hosting the productive activities of foreign MNEs. On the one hand, the dominant theory emphasised the positive effects of the presence of foreign companies on the national territory, pointing out the pro-competitive effects of the economy's greater openness to international competition, and identifying various kinds of externalities or technological spillovers which diffuse the technology[1] owned by the foreign firms into the surrounding environment (see e.g. Caves, 1974; Findlay, 1978). On the other hand, a minority view emphasised the possible anti-competitive consequences of the growing market power wielded by the multinationals by virtue of their expansion into other countries (see e.g. Hymer, 1970), or the negative effect on a country's autochthonous development exerted by the transfer of substandard technologies by foreign MNEs (on this see e.g. Moran, 1970; Lall and Streeten, 1977).

More recently, economic debate seems to have relinquished these extreme positions. Rather than the existence of a univocal relation between foreign presence and economic development, the idea is gaining ground that the processes of productive internationalisation may give rise to both virtuous and vicious circles of development in the countries receiving FDI (Cantwell, 1987, 1989; Cantwell and Dunning, 1991). It is likewise contended that technological spillovers do not spring automatically from the foreign presence, as traditionally argued (Koizumi and Kopecky, 1977; Findlay, 1978; Das, 1987); rather, they result from interaction among local firms, foreign MNEs and government policies (Kokko, 1992; Wang and Blomstrom, 1992).

---

[1] It is advisable to clarify the meaning of some of the terms used in this book.

In keeping with current usage, 'technology' means *"the perishable resource comprising knowledge, skills and the means for using and controlling factors of production for producing [...] delivery and maintaining goods and services."* (Robock, 1980, p. 2).

The expression 'diffusion of technology' refers to both the voluntary dissemination of technology by the company that owns it and the dissemination of technological knowledge against the wishes of the company which possesses that knowledge.

This book develops arguments that belong to this more recent analytical approach. Firstly, it recognises that the process of internationalisation of economies involves winners and losers, rather than producing unequivocally positive or negative effects for the industries of the countries concerned. Secondly, it attempts to explain the links among FDI, government policies and industrial development.

The traditional hypothesis — namely that the presence of subsidiaries of foreign MNEs in the domestic industrial system automatically generates productive externalities or spillovers able to enhance the competitiveness of local firms — gives way to the idea that the effects of FDI can be divided into two types. First there are genuine technological spillovers, that is, the set of effects deriving from the diffusion of the foreign firms' technology to local firms due to physical proximity. Second there are the *displacement* effects on local firms resulting from the greater competitive pressure generated by the presence of foreign firms on the national territory.

According to the analysis conducted in the chapters that follow, multiple factors, interrelated within a complex dynamic system, determine the prevalence of one or other of these effects and therefore the consequences of the passive internationalisation of national productive and innovative systems. Perhaps the most salient of these factors are the following: the initial technological gap between domestic and foreign firms, the level and pace of the expansion of the foreign presence in the country, the strength of the market's selective mechanisms, and the existence of government policies designed to encourage the technological development of local firms and to favour technological exchange between the two groups of firms.

If we take account of this interaction among the various components of a dynamic system, we must abandon the linear relations between foreign presence and technological development envisaged by most studies on the topic (e.g. Findlay, 1978; Blomstrom, 1989; Wang and Blomstrom, 1992). A certain level of foreign penetration — measured as the amount of national inputs or outputs controlled by foreign multinational firms — may have contrasting effects according to the values assumed by the binomial technological gap/foreign presence and by the rate of increase of FDI in the country. This is due to the joint impact of these variables on the pace of technological accumulation by domestic firms, in relation both to the exploitation of local lines of technological development and to the possible imitation of technologies used in the plants of the foreign MNEs. Combining with these factors is government policy. Since this is able to influence the innovative effort of domestic firms and/or regulate competitive pressure by controlling the amount of FDI entering the country, it has powerful effects on the ability of local firms to withstand competition by foreign multinationals. The emergence of virtuous or vicious circles in reaction to the internationalisation of productive systems will depend on the domestic firms' ability — by themselves or as a result of *ad hoc* government policies — to maintain the principal variables at values which enable them to minimise the negative effects of the displacement of local firms and to maximise the beneficial effects of the technological spillovers associated with the presence of foreign firms.

## 1.2. THE GROWTH OF THE THEORY OF INTERNATIONAL PRODUCTION

The first analyses of the internationalisation of capital are probably those associated with Marx and Marxist economists (Lenin in particular). The Marxist–Leninist concept of *multinational firm* can be stated in modern terms by saying that it is a firm which seeks (in vain) to escape the contradictions of capitalism through the *internationalisation* of a larger and larger proportion of its production functions and/or the *imperialistic* exploitation of the labour and natural resources possessed by foreign countries.

In the Marxist approach, the driving force of the internationalisation process is the tendency of the rate of profit to fall in advanced economies, because of the high capital intensity reached by production process and/or increasing labour costs brought by well organised labour unions. This spurs firms from those countries to invest in less developed countries were where capital labour ratio is more favourable and there exists weakly organised labour force.

Marx wrote in *Grundrisse*:

> "... [*Capitalism contains an*] endless and limitless drive to go beyond its limiting barrier. Every limit appears as a barrier to overcome."[2]

---

[2] Marx (1859, p. 408).

While Lenin claimed in his famous essay *Imperialism: The Highest Stage of Capitalism*:

"The export of capital greatly affects and accelerates the development of capitalism in those countries to which it is exported. While, therefore, the export of capital may tend to a certain extent to arrest development in the countries exporting capital, it can only do so by expanding and deepening the further development of capitalism throughout the world."[3]

Although Marxist–Leninist theory is able to explain the causes and effects of the internationalisation of firms, it fails to account for several other distinctive aspects of the expansion of multinationals. Among them: the increasing importance of capital flows among developed nations and the increasingly important role of MNEs as the engine of worldwide technological development.

In the latter respect, further light is shed on international production by Schumpeter (1942) and his thesis that innovative activity is concentrated in the research and development (R&D) laboratories of the big corporations. The latter, according to the 'mature' Schumpeter — thus termed by Freeman (1990) in contrast to the 'young' Schumpeter, "with his emphasis on the individual innovative entrepreneur" (Schumpeter, 1934) — are the main engine not only of capitalist accumulation but of technological accumulation as well, and therefore of economic development.[4]

Marxist–Leninist and Schumpeterian analysis therefore already sets out the fundamental factors in the expansion of MNEs during the twentieth century: the tendency of capital to pass beyond national borders, and the concentration of an ever greater proportion of the world's productive and innovative capacity into the hands of large firms. However, it was only many years after Schumpeter's work that the first specific studies of multinationals sought to define the concept itself of multinational firm, to identify its distinctive features with

---

[3] Lenin (1939, p. 65).
[4] From this it follows, according to arguments developed previously by Schumpeter (1928), that large firms should be ensured sufficient monopolistic rent to stimulate their innovative activities.

respect to uninational ones, and to examine the consequences of FDI on the countries of both origin and destination.

According to an useful classification made by John Cantwell (1989, 1991) modern theories or approaches of international production can be divided into four groups (market power approach, internalisation approach, macroeconomic development approach and competitive international industry approach) which are worth briefly analysing here. Each of them embraces a wide range of contributions, which share some common theoretical foundations. A further approach to international production, the eclectic paradigm, cannot instead be easily incorporated in any analytical schema since it aims to combine elements of all the four groups.

## Market Power Approach

Hymer's *Doctoral Dissertation*, completed in 1960 and published posthumously in 1976, made a crucial contribution to the analysis of international production. According to Hymer (1960), large firms use international production to increase their market power once the opportunities for expansion on the domestic markets have been exhausted. As a means whereby the market power of large firms is exported to other countries, international production has substantially negative effects on the host economies, since it raises market barriers, increases concentration, and restricts the ability of governments to control the national economy.

Hymer's work is forcefully socio-political in its treatment of the activities of MNEs. The latter, according to Hymer, are among the main factors responsible for socio-economic inequalities among nations. They replicate the hierarchies internal to every firm on a worldwide scale by creating similar relations between parent-companies and their foreign subsidiaries. The multinationals thus ensure that the wealthy classes of the more developed nations — since it is these that constitute the top management of the parent-companies — will maintain control over the economically subordinate ones (Hymer, 1970).

Hymer admits the validity of Schumpeter's thesis of a positive relationship between size of firm and technological innovation,[5]

---

[5] Note that, although the literature usually refers to this relation as the 'Schumpeterian hypothesis' it is more properly attributed to Gailbraith (1971), rather than to

and he states that the internationalisation of production can lead to the realisation of new technological goals. Nevertheless, he stresses, besides the pace of technological progress, account should also be taken of its direction. If the market power of the large firms enables them to impose *their* innovative products on world demand, the outcome may be the less vigorous exploitation of geographically differentiated capabilities for innovation.

There are evident similarities between Hymer's arguments and Marxist and Marxist–Leninist analysis. However, the two theories differ sharply because Hymer, while speaking of the *imperialist* issues arising from the actions of multinational firms, expresses complete faith in the re-equilibrating mechanisms of the neoclassical theory of international trade (Hymer, 1970). For Hymer, international trade and international production are two contrasting forces: the one promotes socio-economic equality among countries, the other destroys it.

Applications of the market power approach to international production are in Savary (1984), Newfarmer (1985), Cowling and Sugden (1987) and to some extent in Chesnais (1988, 1992). An influential marxist analysis of the causes and consequences of increasing market power by large MNEs can be found in the classical work on "monopoly capital" by Baran and Sweezy (1966).

Authors following this line of enquiry share the belief of an anticompetitive effect of MNEs. Cowling and Sugden (1987) also stressed the negative effects of international production onto the distribution of income. Chesnais (1988, 1992) emphasised that the bargaining power of MNEs may pare down the ability of governments to control national economies, as well as MNE entry may jeopardise national productive and innovative systems.

## Internalisation Approach

Internalisation approach is originated in Coase (1937), who identified transaction costs as the reason for the existence and growth of productive organisations. Williamson (1975, 1981, 1985) gave new impetus to the line of inquiry developed by

Schumpeter (1942). What Schumpeter in fact emphasised in *Capitalism, Socialism and Democracy* was the relationship between market power and innovation. For further comments see Kamien and Schwartz (1982).

Coase, and Buckley and Casson (1976) applied it to the case of international production.[6]

Under the transaction cost approach, just as in domestic markets firms must choose between centralising their productive, commercial and technological functions under a single management or ownership, and reliance on market transactions for the supply of intermediate inputs, so on foreign markets they are confronted by the choice between FDI, exports or licensing to independent firms. In both cases, the costs and benefits of the alternatives determine the firm's decision, and therefore its size and type (uninational or multinational, for example). Moreover, since FDI involves the transfer not only of capital but of technologies and managerial skills as well (Hymer, 1970), it follows that one of the main reasons for the existence of international production is the presence of market failures in technological transactions (Williamson, 1981).

As recently pointed out by Levy and Dunning (1993), the transaction cost approach is essentially based on the likelihood of opportunism in market transactions. Nevertheless, they observe, fear of opportunism is probably not as widespread as the theory suggests. The Japanese multinationals, for example, have built most of their competitive advantages on the creation of stable long-term relations with their suppliers. This strategy has enabled them to curb opportunism and to create reciprocal trust, if not dependence, in market relationships.[7]

Unlike in the market power approach, advocates of the internalisation theory trust the existence of beneficial effects coming from the growth of MNEs. Even if, in some cases, welfare losses might arise as a consequence of the strategies of profit maximisation pursued by MNEs, which might suggest to restrict output or to raise market barriers, in the large number of cases, the search for efficient transactions (both in the internal and external markets) will enhance R&D expenditure and the development of new products (Buckley, 1985).

---

[6] Buckley and Casson, in fact, were not the first to apply transaction cost theory to international production, but it was their study that established the credentials of this school of thought. Hymer (1968) and McManus (1972) had already investigated international production on the basis of transaction cost theory. See Casson (1991).

[7] For further criticisms of the transaction cost approach see Chapter 7.

## Macroeconomic Development Approach

For various reasons, Vernon's (1966) product cycle hypothesis differed substantially from the theories discussed so far. First, it sought to explain international trade, rather than international production, by means of an approach alternative to the neoclassical theory. Second, as Vernon himself later acknowledged (Vernon, 1979), its explanatory capacity was in part restricted to the postwar period, when the United States enjoyed absolute supremacy in the creation and diffusion of technology and in international production. Third, it comprised an explicit, though no longer fashionable, theory of technological innovation.

The first version of Vernon's product cycle hypothesis (1966) rests on the assumption that each phase in the development of a product (introduction, maturity and standardisation) has a different technological content and requires different inputs in diverse proportions.

Proximity to the final market, and the flexibility and quality of the supply of the production factors, crucially influence the initial phases of product development. Consequently, the American market with its highly skilled human resources, abundance of capital and scientific and technological infrastructures, and with its sophisticated final demand able to absorb the new product but also to provide valuable feedback, was the natural location for the firms of any nation wishing to begin production of a technologically innovative product.

After some time, a certain degree of product standardisation takes place. In this phase, the need for productive flexibility diminishes while production costs grow in importance. Demand, initially concentrated in the USA, now increases in other developed markets (Europe in particular). Production tends to move from the USA to these countries in order to benefit from cheaper production factors and lower transport costs, and in order to circumvent trade barriers.

When the product becomes entirely standardised, the relative importance of production costs increases more than that of the technological factors. Consequently, the less developed countries become the natural location for productive activity.

The product cycle hypothesis has been judged unable to explain the most recent phases of international production for several reasons.[8] In particular, the USA no longer enjoys

---

[8] For more detailed discussion see Cantwell (1989, 1995b).

undisputed technological supremacy; nor indeed can any other countries claim such supremacy. Nor can innovative processes be straightforwardly divided into different phases; nor, moreover, is international production invariably associated with lower technological content. On the contrary, technological innovation is an on-going process which follows distinct technological trajectories and rests on patterns of technological accumulation specific to the firm or to the productive locality (and not to the product), and on oligopolistic reactions.

Close to the Vernon's approach, but developed mainly within the Heckscher–Ohlin–Samuelson model, is the work by Kojima and Ozawa (Kojima, 1978; Kojima and Ozawa, 1985). According to these authors as a country develops, it tends to relocate abroad those productions in which it has a comparative disadvantage and to concentrate resources on more technologically advanced goods. As in the product cycle model, a country involvement in international production follows the process of industrial restructuring at home.

Another approach linking the stages of growth to the FDI path is the investment–development cycle suggested by Dunning (1982). In this case, it is asserted that: (a) the structural changes that an economy undergoes as it growths affect both the level of inward and outward FDI; (b) the FDI activity interacts dynamically with a country economic structure and influences its pattern of development. An interesting and recent restatement of this framework can be found in Narula (1996).

*Eclectic Paradigm*

The explanations of MNE expansion described so far can be labelled as "general theories of international production." In fact, they aim to explain all aspects of this broad phenomenon. It is this characteristic which made them less and less satisfactory as international production evolved into more complex and often unpredictable forms.

The usefulness of a more flexible and less deterministic theoretical framework able to embrace the changing behaviour of MNEs was clear in the early 1980s to John Dunning. His idea was not to develop a new "theory" of international production. Instead, he aimed to set up a framework able to organically embrace different strands of economic analysis.

Dunning (1981, 1988a,b) argues that the various aspects of international production can be analysed from within a broader theoretical approach. He suggests his 'eclectic paradigm' of international production, which, he maintains, is able to incorporate theoretical developments that, though apparently in conflict, are all useful for understanding of the phenomenon in question. Dunning reconsiders one of Hymer's (1960) insights — that MNEs have to rely on some competitive advantage if they are to compete successfully with local firms able to count on long-standing relations with local markets upstream and downstream of the firm — giving it more precise formulation and incorporating it into a broader theoretical framework.

According to Dunning's eclectic paradigm of international production, the existence and growth of MNEs can be explained by their ability:

1. to create and sustain a set of *ownership advantages* deriving either from their sole possession of technologies, technical and managerial skills, and other tangible or intangible assets, or from preferential access to particular markets;
2. to make better use of these advantages, by extending their productive chain or by selling rights for its use to others (*internalisation advantages*);
3. to choose the best location for their exploitation (*locational advantages*).

Although it is true, Dunning argues, that the competitiveness of a firm depends on its ability to produce the type of product that consumers want to buy (or on its ability to persuade them to want to) and to organise production so that production and transaction costs are minimised, it is also true that the efficiency of the productive or commercial process depends on locational choices. Consequently, decisions about what to produce, where to produce, and how to organise production, are the three crucial choices that determine the competitiveness of a firm.

The extraordinary relevance of the eclectic paradigm seems to stem less from its actual formulation than from the extreme flexibility with which Dunning uses it in his empirical investigation of the interaction between international production, on the one hand, and the competitiveness of firms and national production systems on the other.[9] The MNEs exploit the

---

[9] Dunning himself writes: "*It is accepted that, precisely because of its generality, the eclectic paradigm has only a limited power to explain or predict particular kinds of international production; and even less, the behaviour of individual enterprises*" (Dunning, 1988b, p. 41).

opportunities afforded by different productive locations on a world scale, and they contribute to the creation and evolution of locational advantages. The internationalisation of production shapes the competitiveness not only of the MNEs but also of all the firms within their sphere of influence, whether they be rivals, suppliers or buyers, resident in the countries of origin or destination.

## Competitive International Industry Approach

A new stream of analysis which has been growing since the late 1970s is called the "competitive international industry approach." This approach is characterised by the idea that *"the growth of international production tends to be associated with rivalry and to sustain the process of technological competition amongst MNEs."*[10] With respect to the market power approach, which shares the same emphasis on oligopolistic reaction as a driving force of MNE expansion, the competitive international industry approach reaches often opposite conclusions. Rivalry and cooperation between MNEs coming from different countries might act, under certain circumstances, as a stimulus to further technological progress.

The origin of this strand of analysis dates back to the late 1970s when the early version of the product cycle model failed to predict the new developments in the MNE activity. A later development of the product cycle model (Vernon, 1979) and other studies during the 1970s and the 1980s began to stress the role of oligopolistic rivalry as the driving force of internationalisation processes. In the revised version of his product-cycle model (PCM Mark II), Vernon emphasised the role of the threat of price-cutting by rival firms as the key factor justifying the desire of moving away production from mature oligopolistic markets (Vernon, 1974). The work by Graham (1975, 1978, 1985) also highlighted the role played by the exchange of threats in the process of MNE expansion.

A major contribution to the development of this approach has been given by the work by John Cantwell. Moving from Dunning's eclectic paradigm, Cantwell pointed out, the importance of the technological dimension and technological rivalry in analysis of international production (Cantwell, 1989). According to Cantwell, what the eclectic paradigm lacks is an explicit

---

[10] Cantwell (1991, p. 30).

theory of technological innovation (Cantwell, 1992a). Although Dunning (1988a) makes important progress in this direction, Cantwell's (1989) study is the first specific contribution to this area after Vernon's pioneering work (1966).

Sharing the view of Graham (1985) that cross-industry investment arising from rivalry may act as a spur to new product development. Cantwell observes that technological progress is never either entirely embodied or non-embodied in capital goods. Instead, every technological innovation consists of a package of interrelated assets: human capital, tangible and intangible assets. Consequently, the theory of capitalist accumulation and the theory of technological accumulation are two sides of the same coin, and the expansion of the MNEs *"can be linked to a process of cumulative technological change, in which innovation and the growth of international production are mutually supportive."*[11]

Since capitalist and technological accumulation takes place internally to production organisations and locations, the attractiveness of the latter, that is, their locational advantages, will depend *ceteris paribus* on the historical process of accumulation specific to the locality concerned. Hence technology-intense production will tend to concentrate in already highly developed areas, whereas areas characterised by more modest technological development will tend to attract simpler and more standardised production phases.

In his article of 1987, Cantwell assumes that there is a long-period cumulative process whereby international production is tied to the success or failure of productive locations. In areas where technological skills are well-developed, "success breeds success", and virtuous circles of FDI/technological development come about (Cantwell, 1987). Conversely, in areas with scant technological tradition, domestic firms *"fall further and further behind and are generally driven out of world markets in a vicious circle of cumulative decline."*[12,13]

---

[11] Cantwell (1989, p. 7).

[12] Two well-documented examples of virtuous and vicious circles of development are provided by the recent evolution of the British car and pharmaceutical industries. See on this Cantwell (1987, 1993), Dunning (1988a), Cantwell and Sanna Randaccio (1992).

[13] As Cantwell himself has acknowledged (Cantwell, 1989), the arguments set out in the main text fail to explain all the aspects of international production. The internationalisation of firms operates to some extent independently of the exploitation of

The subject of the technological interaction between home and host countries induced by MNEs activities is also developed by Chesnais (1988, 1992). Combining arguments from the market power approach with the modern studies on technological competition, he analysed the effects of MNE activities on the development of national systems of innovation.

Many of the recent studies on the globalisation of economic activities also share many elements developed by this approach. A wider discussion on the new developments in the theory of international production is contained in Chapter 7.

## 1.3. THE ORGANISATION OF THIS BOOK

The next two chapters of this book discuss theoretical questions that are partly resumed in the conclusions (Chapter 7). Chapters 4–6 are instead devoted to analysis of the empirical evidence.

Chapter 2 takes up and develops a number of the arguments treated in the introduction. With its focus on technological spillovers, the chapter conducts a broad survey of the theoretical and empirical literature on the subject. It is this critical re-examination of the literature that provides the basis for the analysis set out in Chapter 3, which is the core of the book and presents the analytical framework for the empirical inquiry in the chapters than follow. The first part of the chapter highlights the main shortcomings of current theoretical models and empirical analyses. The focus then shifts to formulation of alternative models able to generate both vicious and virtuous circles of development. Accordingly, a dynamic model is constructed which takes account of the ambivalent effects of FDI. This model adopts an evolutionary approach which emphasises the

---

ownership and/or technological advantages. It may be driven by the desire to create a more rational international division of labour on the basis of the comparative advantages offered by different productive locations, and/or it may be intended to create competitive advantages for the firm, rather than result from them. Moreover, the internationalisation of local industry, or virtuous circles of development generated by the presence of foreign MNEs, can be observed even in national industrial sectors characterised by low levels of technological development. This is due to the fact that intersectoral differences in the technological development of local industry often conceal major strengths of national industry at the level of industrial district, individual firm, or product line.

interaction that takes place among the processes of industrial selection and learning triggered or accelerated by the presence of foreign firms on the national territory. It is this interaction, it is argued, that determines the development path of domestic industry.

Chapter 4 discusses the reallocation of production factors and innovative activities undertaken in the 1980s and early 1990s by American and Japanese firms in Europe. The analysis reveals that firms of these two countries involve themselves in the productive and innovative systems of the host countries to widely varying extents, apparently in order to reproduce and perpetuate existing disequilibria among the European countries. France, Germany and Great Britain alone attract more than 50% of productive and innovative activity by American and Japanese firms in Europe; Italy, Spain, Greece and Portugal less than 10%. Moreover, analysis of the sectoral composition of productive and innovative activity by American and Japanese multinationals highlights the decisive role played by the strengths and weaknesses of national systems in the passive internationalisation of the economies of the European countries, especially as regards the technological content of the activities undertaken by foreign multinationals on national territory. Finally, with reference to the American multinationals, the empirical analysis shows that the trade-off between local production and the importing of technology works in favour of the former in the European countries with longer traditions as the basis for FDI by American firms. This finding apparently confirms the evolutionary tendency of the foreign subsidiaries of MNEs to grow increasingly independent of their parent-companies in satisfying of their technological needs (Cantwell, 1989).

Moving from the general to the particular, Chapters 5 and 6 examine two national cases: the manufacturing industries of Britain and Italy. As regards the former, the empirical evidence — on eighteen manufacturing sectors at two moments of time, 1983 and 1989 — confirm the occurrence in that country of rapid virtuous and vicious circles of development consequent on the marked expansion of the foreign presence in British industry during the 1980s. The *laissez-faire* industrial policies pursued by Conservative governments in those years, and the measures introduced to attract FDI (promotional activities and tax concessions and benefits for foreign investors), seemingly accentuated the strengths and weaknesses of domestic industry. In sectors where, technologically, British firms initially lagged far behind their main international competitors, their market shares were further reduced while the technological gap widened. Conversely, in sectors where the initial differences were less marked, the performance of British firms was much better in terms of both growth of output and of labour productivity.

The link between the technological competence of domestic firms and the consequences of the presence of foreign firms is also evident in Italian manufacturing industry. The data on Italy have been taken from a sample of more than 4000 firms contained in the *Mediocredito Centrale* data bank for 1991 (Mediocredito Centrale, 1994) and compared with the figures on the foreign presence in Italian industry contained in the *Ricerche e Progetti* data bank (Cominotti and Mariotti, various years). They show that the effect of the foreign presence on the dispersion of productivity in each productive sector is related to the strengths and weaknesses of Italian industry. In fact, leaving traditional sectors aside — given that they do not exhibit significant relations, probably because of the insignificant presence of foreign firms — the effects of the Italian economy's passive internationalisation on labour productivity in domestic firms are positive in scale-intensive sectors (specialist ones especially) and negative in science-based sectors.

Chapter 7 resumes some of the topics already treated in previous chapters in order to examine the interrelations among the various forms assumed by the active and passive internationalisation of national economies. The aim is to suggest further directions of research in this area, and to provide a brief description of certain recent theoretical developments and their possible extension.

I conclude these introductory remarks by pointing out some of the limitations to this book.

First, since only one of the many aspects of productive internationalisation (the impact of FDI on the technological development of local firms) is analysed, the links among the various components of the process are neglected. As discussed in more detail in the conclusions (Chapter 7), it is my opinion that, in each development phase of a productive system, international trade and incoming and outgoing FDI, as well as international cooperation agreements between resident and non-resident firms, are closely interrelated phenomena, since they jointly express the characteristics and the attractiveness of the national innovative and productive system (Narula and Wakelin, 1995), and they are also the principal determinants of its future development.

Secondly, the data available for the analysis conducted in this book have not permitted detailed examination of the diffusion of technology which distinguishes the influence exerted on this process by the type of technology transferred abroad or by the various strategies pursued by the MNEs. As already emphasised by other authors (for example, Kokko, 1992), both these features should be discussed in more thoroughgoing study of the technology diffusion engendered by FDI.

Moreover, again because of the limits imposed by the availability of data, the econometric analyses set out in Chapters 5 and 6 concentrate on intra-sectoral spillovers, entirely ignoring those that occur among groups of vertically linked firms. As evidenced by the almost total lack of studies in this area, intersectoral spillovers are difficult to analyse empirically — but no less important because of this, given that many technology diffusion processes probably stem from the technical assistance provided by the subsidiaries of foreign MNEs to the domestic firms supplying them with parts and components.[14]

---

[14] For empirical data concerning the British case see Dunning (1958) and Strange (1993).

# 2. MNEs and Technological Spillovers: A Survey

## 2.1. INTRODUCTION

Analysis of the relationship between the internationalisation of production and the economic development of the recipient nations has attracted the attention of many economists over the last decades. As the main engine of this process, the birth and subsequent rapid growth of MNEs has likewise been the focus of considerable analytical effort. Not only are these firms universally regarded as possessing the technological knowledge necessary for economic development, they are seen as the foremost agencies of the international diffusion of these technologies, or, conversely, as a major obstacle against the industrial take-off of the countries that receive FDI.

Since the first Marxist and Leninist analyses of the internationalisation of capital, rivers of ink have been spilled in arguing one or other of these positions, prompting heated economic and political debate. Nor, moreover, do the changing forms assumed by the internationalisation or globalisation of the economy presage any imminent end to argument on the matter.

The following sections will concentrate on the implications of international production for the competitiveness of the nations receiving FDI. The focus in particular will be on the ways in which the presence of the subsidiaries of foreign MNEs may affect the technological development of the indigenous industrial system. The analysis proposed will seek to be something more than a straightforward review of the literature on the topic. I shall try, in fact, to offer a critical account of the existing literature, endeavouring to identify its main weaknesses or limitations and thereby mark out the areas on which the analysis developed in later chapters will concentrate.

Section 2.2 discusses the role of MNEs in the creation and international transfer of technology. Also analysed will be the various ways in which FDI may enhance the international competitiveness of the recipient industrial systems, distinguishing between direct and indirect effects, and, within this latter category, between processes which displace less competitive local firms and those that diffuse technology. The theme of the transfer of technology by the subsidiaries of foreign MNEs to domestic firms will be resumed and expanded in subsequent sections, which discuss the various types of technological spillovers (Section 2.3), the environmental factors that favour their genesis (Section 2.4), the main theoretical models on the topic (Section 2.5) and the results of empirical studies (Section 2.6). A number of brief conclusions are drawn in Section 2.7.

## 2.2. MNES AND TECHNOLOGY: THE KEY RELATIONS

As early as 1971, Keith Pavitt pointed out that:

> "... technology and the MNE are mutually dependent. Most of industrial R&D is performed in large — and therefore multinational — firms."[1]

He estimated that, in eight developed economies, between 30% and 50% of all spending on R&D in the private sector was made by the top eight firms in terms of sales volume. More recently, Patel and Pavitt (1991) have calculated that, between 1981 and 1986, the 686 largest firms in the world registered 49% of all patents in the USA, and 60% of those by firms. On the other hand, if technological activity is closely concentrated in the large firms,[2] so too is the international transfer of technology. In the USA between 1986 and 1990, more than 75%

---

[1] Pavitt (1971, p. 61).

[2] The figures probably overestimate the importance of large firms. For obvious computational problems, technological activity by small and medium-sized firms, which frequently does not result in patents on the American market or in formal R&D, is entirely ignored by this type of analysis.

of all technology receipts came from the foreign subsidiaries of American MNEs, while in Germany the figure was higher than 90% (UNCTC, 1992). Consequently, the MNEs are important for at least two reasons: as the possessors of the bulk of technological knowledge and skills, and as the principal agencies of the international transfer of such knowledge and skills.

The international transfer of technology may come about in various ways: international trade in capital goods and manufactures, licensing to independent foreign firms or to foreign subsidiaries, and FDI. Compared with market transactions (licensing and international trade among independent firms), FDI displays three distinctive features. First, ownership of capital goods and technologies remains in the hands of the transferor. Second, FDI normally involves the transfer of a package of interrelated technologies consisting of machinery, capital equipment, blueprints, company trademarks and managerial skills. Third, owing to the difficulty of transferring technological innovations as yet not fully codified (Teece, 1977), and to the risk of losing important ownership advantages, the transfer of technology within the same productive organisation usually involves technologies much newer than those transferred among independent firms (Mansfield and Romeo, 1980).

If we exclude the case of erroneous decisions taken by the MNE undertaking the operation, the international transfer of technology via FDI is primarily to the benefit of the competitiveness of the MNE itself. By exploiting the locational advantages offered by diverse production sites, the multinational company increases its competitive advantage over rival firms. Thanks to the long-term relations between foreign subsidiaries and the parent-company, the latter is able to internalise the feedback from the new application of its technology in a different environment.[3]

The impact of FDI, however, is not exhausted internally to the MNE. On the contrary, according to numerous authors, its repercussions externally to the firm's productive network are

---

[3] As Teece (1977) notes, every new start-up increases the firm's knowledge about the technology being transferred. Dunning (1988a) points out that these feedbacks are presumably maximised when there exists a long-standing relationship between transferor and transferee, as in the case of transfers from the parent-company to foreign subsidiaries.

much more important, both in the nations of origin and in those receiving the FDI.

Restricting the analysis to the recipient nations, in discussion of the effect of MNEs on the international diffusion of technology a useful distinction can be drawn between *direct effects* and *indirect effects* or *spillovers*.[4]

As regards direct effects, whenever a MNE sets up a plant in a foreign country, it transfers part of its technology. Consequently, FDI is in the first place associated with an increase in the technological knowledge and skills *resident* in the destination country, although this does not imply any change in the ownership or control of such activities.

The broad category of indirect effects comprises all those phenomena tied to the presence of foreign firms on the national territory that may increase the productive efficiency of domestic firms or their innovative capacity. Since these effects are not normally desired by the MNE making the investment, because the resulting benefits are not fully appropriated by it, from an economic point of view they belong to the area of *externalities* and are currently indicated in the literature as *productivity spillovers*.[5]

The spillovers created by the activity of foreign MNEs and directed towards local firms may be of various kinds, and they may affect companies vertically connected with the MNE (*inter-industry spillovers*) or in direct competition with it (*intra-industry spillovers*). Or they may affect the entire productive structure of the host country by encouraging, for example, the better allocation of resources among production sectors.

Although it is often empirically difficult to discriminate among the various types of spillovers, from a methodological point of view it is advisable to distinguish the broad category

---

[4] Of course, FDI has direct and indirect effects in areas other than that of technology diffusion. For example, every greenfield investment by a MNE *directly* increases total employment in the host country, albeit with possible negative effects on employment in rival domestic firms. But it may also *indirectly* increase employment by means of Keynesian multiplier effects. Similarly, FDI produces direct and indirect effects on the Balance of Payment of both the investing and the recipient countries.

[5] Regarding the character of productivity spillovers, Caves (1974, p. 176) notes that they occur whenever "... [the] *multinational corporation cannot capture all quasi-rents due to its productive activities, or to the removal of distortions by the subsidiary's competitive pressure.*"

of *productivity spillovers* from the sub-set of *technological spillovers*. Whereas the former occur whenever the presence of foreign firms on the national territory produces an increase in the *average productivity* of domestic firms, the latter requires that this increase should be associated with an improvement in the techniques used by local firms.[6]

A brief example may help to clarify the distinction. The average productivity of local firms may increase because the greater competition generated by the presence of subsidiaries of foreign MNEs pushes less efficient domestic firms out of the market. The resources thus freed may be absorbed by other domestic firms in other sectors, thereby causing a further increase in the average productivity of the national productive system. In this case, productivity spillovers will occur, but not technological spillovers. Conversely, productivity spillovers may be associated with technological spillovers when the presence of MNEs on the national territory brings an improvement in the technology used by domestic firms, because technology spreads from the plants of the subsidiaries of the foreign MNEs to the surrounding environment, and/or because the greater competitive pressure perceived by local firms induces them to devote greater resources to improving their competitiveness. The two phenomena are often associated in practice, since both processes of industrial restructuring (the market exit of less efficient domestic firms) and processes of company-level restructuring (the increased efforts made by the surviving firms to improve their competitiveness) are likely to be connected with changes in competitive conditions.

In what follows, unless indicated otherwise, the term 'spillovers' will be used to denote only technological spillovers, since

---

[6] This distinction is not explicitly drawn in the literature but emerges from close analysis. The overwhelming majority of authors talk of technological spillovers, referring to possible technological advances in domestic firms brought about by the presence of foreign firms. An exception is Caves (1974), who uses the term spillovers of productivity but distinguishes between allocative efficiency benefits which may originate from the fact that MNEs entering industries characterised by high barriers to entry "may pare down monopolistic distortions and raise productivity of the host country's resources their allocation" (p. 176), on the one hand, and technical efficiency and technological transfer on the other. Also Blomstrom and Wolff (1989, 1993) draw a distinction between technological spillovers and the improvements in the average productivity of domestic firms deriving from the closure of the less competitive ones. Kokko (1992) instead gets round the problem by treating the two terms as interchangeable.

it is these that are most germane to my analysis of technology diffusion. However, it will become clear, both in the survey of the literature conducted in this chapter and in the empirical inquiry developed in subsequent ones, that for practical purposes it is difficult to draw a sharp distinction between the two phenomena. However, the model developed in Chapter 3 will further clarify the distinctions and interrelations between the various kinds of spillovers, as well as highlighting their various implications for the competitiveness of the country receiving FDI.

Furthermore, I shall for the moment ignore the direct effects of the presence of MNEs on the technological capacity and knowledge of the country that receives FDI, returning to the topic in later chapters.

## 2.3. TECHNOLOGICAL SPILLOVERS: POSSIBLE TYPES

The technological spillovers from the activity of foreign MNEs to local firms may assume different forms.[7]

First, the presence of foreign MNEs usually increases competitive pressure on local markets (*competition-related spillovers*). By upsetting previous market equilibria, foreign MNEs stimulate local firms to increase their productivity and/or introduce product innovations in order to defend their market shares.

These effects may be particularly important in industries characterised by a low level of actual or potential competition which provides scant stimulus to firms to reduce costs or improve their products. Belonging to this category are sectors characterised by high commercial barriers or high transport costs, which inhibit competition by foreign firms in the absence of productive activity *in loco*, or those characterised by high barriers to entry which are easily circumvented by MNEs thanks to their high technological and financial capacity.

The effects of spillovers deriving from competition between local firms and foreign multinationals are not restricted to the moment of the latters' entry into the national industrial system. On the contrary, spillovers express their full potential when they are embodied in the virtuous dynamics generated by

---

[7] See Blomstrom (1989, 1991) and Kokko (1992) for similar classifications.

technological competition between domestic and foreign firms, which impel them to improve their product and process technologies in order to defend their market shares.

The bulk of the literature tends towards the pro-competitive effect of FDI, emphasising its role in removing oligopolist barriers and in upsetting previous market equilibria.[8] However, there are a number of dissenting opinions that warrant examination. First, from a general point of view, the relationship between market concentration and technical progress is anything but proven. Cantwell (1989), for example, argues forcefully that a higher level of technological competition may be associated with both increasing and decreasing indices of market concentration. Rather, it is the reactive capacity of the domestic firms — which depends, amongst other things, on the technical competence developed prior to the arrival of the foreign MNEs — that determines the positive or negative sign of international production on the competitiveness of the countries receiving FDI. Second, as Hymer (1960, 1970) has pointed out, MNEs are often themselves the cause of oligopolist distortions. By moving productive activities, financial capital and marketing skills around the world, the big corporations export and internationalise their market power and monopolise channels of distribution. Moreover, the internationalisation of production may not only break up existing oligopolist equilibria but also dismantle the vertical and horizontal linkages among domestic firms and/or between productive sectors and the national institutions. It thus reduces the cohesion, and therefore the competitive capacity, of the national system of production and innovation, and this outcome is particularly damaging to the small and medium-sized firms unable to exploit the advantages of the internationalisation of production (Chesnais, 1992).

A second type of spillovers concern the technical and managerial cooperation that may occur between the foreign subsidiaries of the multinational corporations and local firms, whether these are located upstream or downstream of the productive activity of the foreign companies, or whether they are competing firms. A number of case studies have shown that when MNEs establish new plants in a foreign country, they commit resources to improving the technological competence of

---

[8] See Kindleberger (1969), Caves (1974), Blomstrom (1989) and Kokko (1992) and other works by these authors listed in the bibliography.

the vertically or horizontally linked local firms, thus ensuring that these meet the requirements of the subsidiaries in terms of quality standards, work schedules, and so on.

Dunning (1958) was the first to stress the importance of this kind of cooperation between subsidiaries and local firms on the basis of a questionnaire administered to the subsidiaries of American firms in the United Kingdom.[9] Not only did the American MNEs establish cooperative relations with their local suppliers by providing various kinds of technical assistance, they were also *"at the forefront of schemes to develop a freer interchange of knowledge between firms in the UK, and frequently organised exchanges and welcomed visits by the managerial and technical staff of their major rivals."*[10]

Whether these kinds of relations characterise the behaviour of MNEs in general is certainly a matter for discussion and further empirical verification. Studies of Japanese MNEs, for example, suggest that they tend to continue with their customary suppliers, rather than use local producers. Where there exist local content regulations, or managerial practices which require physical proximity between the foreign subsidiaries and its suppliers (*just-in-time delivery systems*, for example), one of the chief strategies of Japanese firms is to encourage their usual Japanese suppliers to set up production units in countries receiving FDI.[11] More in general, Cantwell (1989) suggests that the foreign subsidiaries of MNEs tend, with the passage of time, to intensify their vertical relations with local firms and to establish more stable linkages with the local environment.[12]

Among the most frequently cited forms of technology diffusion are the *human capital spillovers* whereby the technological and managerial skills acquired from on-the-job training in the production plants of MNEs can be utilised by local firms, or may give rise to new production units. Blomstrom (1991) argues that these spillovers are especially important in developing countries, given their lack of trained labour and managerial skills. However, the difficult codifiability of certain forms of

---

[9] See also the excellent survey of Dunning's work in Cantwell (1992a) and the other essays collected in Buckley and Casson (1992).

[10] Cantwell (1992a, p. 33).

[11] See on this Graham and Krugman (1989) and Levy and Dunning (1993).

[12] For empirical evidence on this phenomenon see Safarian (1966), Forsyth (1972), McAleese and McDonald (1978), Dunning (1986).

technical and managerial knowledge suggests that human factor mobility between foreign and domestic firms might contribute substantially to the technological development of local firms in the industrialised countries as well, although the total lack of empirical studies precludes any definitive conclusion on the matter.

Whatever the case may be, the importance of flows of human capital to productive networks competing with those of the MNEs that have generated them should not be overestimated. As Pavitt (1971) points out, although it is true that:

"... many of the small firms that have exploited radical innovations have been started, or greatly assisted, by scientists and engineers with previous work experience in the laboratories of large firms"

it is also true that

"... large firms are very often customers for the products of these small firms when they start."[13]

A last group of spillovers identified by the literature comprises what are known as *demonstration-* and *imitation-type spillovers*. Owing to their similarity (indeed they are very often not clearly distinguishable), these will be treated jointly here. On the one hand, the presence of production units established by foreign multinationals may demonstrate to local firms that a certain type of production or particular productive and organisational methods may be realised with success even in the socio-economic conditions of the country receiving FDI (*demonstration-type spillovers*). On the other hand, the proximity of foreign MNEs to local firms may encourage the latter to imitate the technologies utilised in the foreign firms by means of reverse engineering, personal contacts or industrial espionage (*imitation-type spillovers*).

## 2.4. THE CONDITIONS FAVOURING TECHNOLOGICAL SPILLOVERS

The magnitude of possible technological spillovers from the subsidiaries of foreign MNEs to local firms depends on numerous

---

[13] Pavitt (1971, p. 62).

and often interrelated factors. Those most frequently mentioned in the literature are the following: the type of technology transferred by MNEs in the host country; the strategies pursued by these firms in undertaking productive internationalisation; the degree to which the productive activity of their foreign subsidiaries is integrated with the local productive system; the ability of local firms to absorb or stimulate technological spillovers; government policies towards FDI.

The type of technology transferred from the parent company to its affiliates abroad, and its possible inadequacy *vis-à-vis* the needs of the destination countries, has always been an major issue in debate on the consequences of international production. In the 1950s and 1960s an influential current of thought, originating in South America and known as the 'school of the *dependencia*', repeatedly stressed that the excessively intense use of capital by the subsidiaries of the American MNEs made it impossible for technology to spread to local firms, since these did not have the necessary financial support and were unable to grow to the size required for the efficient use of these productive methods. While this was happening, FDI exacerbated unemployment and forced the closure of local firms which, although dynamic, still fell well short of the technological and capitalist level of the foreign multinationals.[14]

Similar arguments have been more recently put forward concerning the effects of direct American investments, when compared with investments by Japanese firms. Fujita and Hill (1995), for example, maintain that American investment based on Fordist production methods — i.e. on the use of unskilled labour subservient to specific machinery and on rigid hierarchical relations — has scant effect on the spread of technology to the surrounding environment. By contrast, establishment of production units like those of the Japanese multinationals, characterised by a skilled workforce operating versatile machinery and by cooperative relations between management and workers, would, in Fujita and Hill's opinion, give rise to a potentially high transfer of human capital to the external environment.

Analysis of organisational and managerial aspects should not overlook the degree of novelty of the technology transferred, in

---

[14] For a critical examination of this and other claims by the school of the *dependencia* see Moran (1970).

all cases where this can be classified on a scale ranging from the most mature technologies to the most innovative ones. As regards the former aspect, all the empirical analyse available show that the transfer of technology among different plants of a MNE is strongly influenced by the degree of development of the recipient nation. For example, Mansfield and Romeo (1980) report that, in their sample of 31 multinational American firms, the transfer of technologies among plants belonging to the same firm took place almost six years after the first application of the technology by the parent company in the case of affiliates in developed countries, and after around thirteen years in the case of affiliates in developing countries. Kokko (1992) and Blomstrom and Kokko (1993) analyse the foreign operations of American MNEs in 33 countries in 1982 to show that payments for patents and technology licences by foreign subsidiaries were positively correlated with the rates of university education in the countries considered.[15] Surveys of the behaviour by the subsidiaries of foreign multinationals operating in Mexico have produced similar results, evidencing a close causal connection between the competitiveness of local industry and the importing of technology by foreign firms (Kokko, 1992; Blomstrom, Kokko and Zejan, 1992).

The type and novelty of the technology transferred highlight the importance of the second aspect of the problem, namely the strategy pursued by MNEs in undertaking multinationalisation. The modern processes of the *rationalisation* and the *globalisation* of production indicate, albeit with different implications, a shift in the organisational patterns of international production towards the greater specialisation of productive areas. Compared with the strategy pursued in the previous phase of expansion in international production, based on the creation of plants operating entirely or almost entirely independently of the other production units of the multinational group, production rationalisation and globalisation are processes both of which entail the dispersion of the various phases of a value added chain among several plants which, although

---

[15] Kokko (1992) also points out a negative correlation between the rate of productivity growth in the foreign subsidiaries between 1977 and 1982 and the technological gap between local and American industry. In both the studies cited in the main text the figure refer to the whole of the manufacturing sector.

internationally scattered, are integrated by intra-firm trade. However, rationalisation and globalisation differ according to the amount of independence accorded to each link in the chain, which is very limited in the former case and very marked in the latter.

The rigid division of the various phases of the production process (design, production of components, assembly, etc.) typical of rationalised firms is replicated in the allocation of productive activities among countries according to their levels of development. Because of their low labour costs, the more backward countries become centres for the assembly of technological evolved intermediate goods designed and produced in the more developed countries, and this reproduces and exacerbates already-existing disparities. By contrast, in the case of the global centres of production or R&D, the co-equal role assigned to each unit in the building of the company's competitive advantages and in the use of corporate resources should, at least in theory, increase spillovers and favour the integration of the less developed countries into the process of technological development of the more advanced ones.

It should be stressed, however, that the existence of substantially different effects between the two types of investment has not been empirically demonstrated, and that there are no discernible trends that argue clearly in favour of one form of productive internationalisation rather than the other. In North America, for example, whilst the Ford motor company has delegated the design of its new cars to a highly specialised Mexican centre, numerous other American firms have responded to the creation of the North America Free Trade Agreement (NAFTA) by relocating the standardised phases of their production to southern Mexico, thereby benefiting from low Mexican labour costs.

The importance of the intensity of the links established by the MNEs with firms upstream and downstream of their productive networks have already been discussed in the previous section. In this connection, a widely held and plausible argument maintains that the greater the integration of the foreign subsidiaries of MNEs into the national productive system, the greater the potential flows of technological knowledge from foreign to local firms.

Lall (1978) was among the first to clarify the crucial role played by vertical links with the local firms set up by the multinationals, with particular reference to the developing countries:

"The 'direct' relationship that transnational corporations strike up with local suppliers or purchasers... can constitute powerful mechanisms for stimulating (or retarding) economic, and particularly industrial, growth in LDCs."[16]

Moreover, according to Lall, the frequently used strategy of calculating the local content of production as a proxy for the beneficial effects of FDI is less than satisfactory. From both an economic and social point of view, costs and benefits should be carefully weighed, taking account of the alternatives available and of the possible depressive effects of entry by foreign multinationals on the growth of the local industrial system. Although Lall's remarks most closely concern the developing countries, where foreign investment may be the first "unbalancing step"[17] towards industrial take-off via the creation of external economies in vertically connected sectors, there is no reason why, *mutatis mutandis*, they should not also apply to the more developed economies.

Dunning (1986), for example, reports the complaints of some local suppliers to Japanese firms in Great Britain that the products ordered from them were designed for techniques specific to Japanese companies, and that local firms could not achieve sufficient scale economies in their production to be competitive. Hence derives the danger that local industry may deviate from the lines of technological development appropriate to it because of the constraints imposed by foreign companies, without their obtaining clear benefits in terms of competitiveness, and indeed running the risk of being left with empty order books should foreign multinationals decide to reallocate their productive activities or more simply to shift their supply of intermediate products to other countries.[18]

---

[16] Lall (1978, p. 217).

[17] The reference is to Hirschman (1958).

[18] To venture a historical parallel, this situation resembles that of the many ex-colonial nations whose economies were transformed to accentuate productive specialisation during their long periods of foreign domination. This was a relatively efficient system (from a purely economic point of view) as long as the country was a colony, but it was disastrous once the country had achieved independence and was obliged to operate on the open market without preferential access to the markets of the ex-coloniser country.

A point made by all recent studies of the factors influencing the impact of foreign MNEs on indigenous industrial systems is the importance of the degree of technological development of local industry in creating conditions favourable for technological spillovers. Both the type of technology transferred and the role assigned to a particular country in the rationalisation or globalisation of production, as well as the quantity and quality of the links established by the subsidiaries of foreign multinationals with local industry, are closely influenced by the development level of the indigenous industrial system, and by its ability to respond positively to the stimuli arising from the foreign presence.

When local firms are technologically backward and with modest levels of human capital, foreign MNEs will tend to transfer production phases with low value added and limited technological content, in order to exploit low labour costs. Vertical links with local firms will be restricted by the inability of local suppliers to fulfil the technological standards required, and the spillovers generated by foreign investment will consequently be minor. By contrast, when productive locations can draw on high-quality human capital and a highly developed and competitive base, MNEs will transfer activities with a high technological content. They will commission technologically advanced intermediate products and components from indigenous firms, and develop complex forms of collaboration with local entrepreneurs. And they will seek to integrate as closely as possible with the local technological and scientific community, thus creating the conditions for substantial flows of technology in both directions.

On the other hand, since the ability of local firms to absorb spillovers also depends largely on their level of technological development, as Cantwell repeatedly stressed (1987, 1989), when local firms can count on high levels of technological accumulation, they are able to deploy their resources in response to the invasion by foreign multinationals, thereby further consolidating and developing their technological advantages. By contrast, when the technological competence of local industry is modest, foreign multinationals will have no difficulty in beating off the local competition, thereby further weakening the country's technological and productive base.

Cantwell sums up the implications of these processes as follows. Given that, *ceteris paribus*, the MNEs tend to tap into local lines of technological development and/or to import more technology to productive locations in which local competition is strongest, existing centres of excellence in the development of a certain technology will benefit most from possible technological spillovers. In these productive areas, in fact, the importing of technology by foreign subsidiaries, and the absorption of foreign technology by local firms, will interact to generate virtuous circles of technological development. Conversely, locations characterised by a lower level of development will receive productions with modest technological content. Of these latter locations, those where domestic firms have some lines of technological development but are not at the technological frontier are the ones most likely to be penalised by the presence of foreign multinationals, since the competitiveness of local firms may be affected by the expansion of the MNEs brought about R&D conducted elsewhere. Locations with little (or no) productive development may instead at least benefit from the increased economic activity. There therefore exists, according to Cantwell, a J-shaped relation between spillovers and the pre-existing level of technological development of locations that receive FDI.

In conclusion to this section on the conditions favouring the technological spillovers deriving from the presence of foreign MNEs, according to the list given earlier there only remains the role of government policies in the countries receiving FDI. Evidently, opinions on this subject diverge sharply, although this contrast is partly due to the different areas addressed by the theories proposed: the developing countries in some cases, the more industrialised ones in others. In brief, one may say that the economic policy measures set out in the literature range from the granting of complete freedom to international movements of production capital and to the activities of MNEs, through efforts to ensure — albeit in full respect for the freedom of international capital flows — that action by foreign MNEs does not hamper the development of the indigenous industrial system, to outright rejection of FDI.

The first category comprises much of the recent literature on models of endogenous growth of neoclassical stamp.[19] These

---

[19] For an application of endogenous growth theory to the technological spillovers generated by MNEs see the Wang and Blomstrom's model (1992) described in Section 2.5.

have provided the basis for recent empirical studies seeking to show the existence of a negative relation between government intervention and technological spillovers. Kokko (1992) and Blomstrom and Kokko (1993), for example, report that the imposition of performance requirements by governments receiving production investments from foreign MNEs reduce the importation of advanced technology by the latter. Balasubramanyam, Salisu and Sapsford (1996) highlight the marked prevalence of positive effects generated by FDI on the rate of growth of per-capita income in developing countries pursuing policies of openness to international markets, compared with those whose governments have adopted import substituting subsidies. The same authors refer to research by Bhagwati (1978, 1985) in order to show that a strategy designed to promote exports by domestic firms, rather than the substitution of imported products, both attracts a larger volume of FDI and creates a climate favourable to productive efficiency, as well as stimulating technological spillovers from the subsidiaries of foreign multinationals to local firms.

A substantially different theoretical framework underpins the positions taken up by those authors who, although they acknowledge the importance of the possible beneficial effects of FDI, also stress that a massive foreign presence may, under certain conditions, trigger the decline of the domestic industrial base (Cantwell, 1987; Cantwell and Dunning, 1991). Although Dunning, for example, emphasises that the available empirical evidence strongly supports the continuation of a *laissez-faire* policy towards the Japanese multinationals operating in Great Britain, he expresses concern that Japanese investments may prove to be a "Trojan horse" for British industry, since these firms may reduce the national technological and productive base while keeping the core of their innovative activities in Japan (Dunning, 1986). The consequence is, firstly, that industrial policies are required which encourage indigenous firms to achieve a level of technological development that enables them to withstand competition by foreign multinationals; and secondly that governments must constantly monitor the activities of foreign MNEs in order to ensure that they do not hamper the industrial development of the country (Dunning, 1985).

Finally, there are those extreme positions which reject FDI on account of various argumentation. Hymer (1970), for instance, argues that since one of the main characteristic of

MNE activity is the monopolistic distortions they generate, the only option available to governments is to try to restrict their freedom of action as much as possible. Baran and Sweezy point out that the MNEs work in their own interest; and that this interest, except in exceptional circumstances, coincides neither with that of the countries of origin nor with that of the destination countries. Any intervention by national governments in order to regulate the activities of the multinationals is therefore to be recommended (Baran and Sweezy, 1966). Similar conclusions are reached by Chesnais analysing the impact of globalisation of production onto national system of innovations. If both the exploitation of the positive externalities or spillovers associated with FDI, and more in general the growth of the national economy, depend on the cohesiveness and development of the domestic productive and innovative system — which by their nature the MNEs of every country tend to by-pass — the best economic policy is not to assign any strategic role to these firms, and if their presence may impede the working of that system, to refuse them entry (Chesnais, 1992).

## 2.5. THEORETICAL MODELS OF TECHNOLOGICAL SPILLOVERS

To my knowledge, Koizumi and Kopecky (1977) were the first to conduct formal analysis of the technological spillovers generated by the presence of subsidiaries of foreign MNEs. In their examination of the relationship between long-period international capital movements and economic development, the authors assume that FDI enables the residents of the host countries to tap into foreign lines of technological development. They write:

> "These new ideas are transmitted from foreigners to residents by observation, discussion and training and tend to permeate throughout the country's economy."[20]

Koizumi and Kopecky view technological spillovers as *public goods* for the country receiving the FDI, and as production *externalities* for the foreign MNEs. Indeed, as Caves (1974)

---

[20] Koizumi and Kopecky (1977, p. 49).

has also stressed, technological spillovers can be exploited by residents free of charge and the MNEs are unable fully to appropriate the returns on them.

Since spillovers increase the technological knowledge of domestic firms, and assuming that the capital stock of the subsidiaries of foreign MNEs ($K_f$) is a good proxy for the transfer of technology by these firms, the aggregate production function of resident firms (i.e. domestic firms and the affiliates of foreign multinationals) can be written as:

$$Q = \Psi\left(\frac{K_f}{L}\right) \cdot G(K_f + K_d, L), \qquad (2.1)$$

where $Q$ denotes output by all the firms in the country, $L$ is labour and $K_d$ is the stock of capital owned by domestic firms. The function $\Psi(K_f/L)$ identifies the technological spillovers, and it assumes values greater than one for $(K_f/L) > 0$. Assuming further that technological spillovers are directly proportional to the foreign presence, one has:

$$\frac{\partial \Psi}{\partial K_f} > 0. \qquad (2.2)$$

This specification of technological spillovers as public goods implies that the marginal returns on 'foreign' capital and on 'national' capital (i.e. the social return on capital) differ. In fact, by differentiating Eq. (2.1) with respect to $K_d$ and $K_f$, we get respectively the marginal social return on national ($RMC_d$) and foreign capital ($RMC_f$):

$$RMC_d = \frac{\partial Q}{\partial K_d} = \Psi G_K, \qquad (2.3)$$

$$RMC_f = \frac{\partial Q}{\partial K_f} = \left(\frac{\partial \Psi}{\partial K_f}\right)G + \Psi G_K, \qquad (2.4)$$

where the term $(\partial \Psi / \partial K_f)G$ measures the externalities associated with the FDI.

Since $RMC_f > RMC_d$, any policy intended to slow down or to diminish foreign penetration into the national economy will give rise to a net reduction in social welfare. Moreover, whereas for the national economy the foreign investment has a greater social return than that realised by domestic investment, the MNEs are unable to appropriate the factor $(\partial \Psi / \partial K_f) G$, and the *private* marginal value of both national and foreign capital will therefore be equal to $\Psi G_K$. This indicates the advantages of policies designed to bring the private marginal return on FDI closer to the social return for the host country, thereby stimulating a greater inflow of foreign capital.

Findlay (1978) refers to the by now classic studies of Veblen and Gerschenkron[21] on catching-up processes among nations at different stages of development. He assumes that, as long as the disparities are not so great that they impede any learning process at all, the greater the technological gap between two nations or regions, the greater will be the opportunities for technological advancement enjoyed by firms resident in the relatively more backward area (the 'convergence hypothesis' or the 'advantages of backwardness hypothesis'). According to Findlay, when the subsidiaries of foreign MNEs make full use of the technological resources of their parent companies, the argument can be extended to the case of FDI in developing nations, or at any rate in countries more backward than those in which these investments originate: the wider the technological gap between foreign subsidiaries and domestic firms, the greater the possible technological spillovers.

Together with this hypothesis, and drawing this time on early studies of technology diffusion (Mansfield, 1961, 1968), Findlay draws an analogy between the spread of technology and the spread of a contagious disease. The basis for his analogy is the fact that the imitation of someone else's technology requires personal contact between the two parties. Besides, since technological knowledge tends to reside in the R&D divisions of the great corporations, as already pointed out by Schumpeter (1942):

"[...] the 'carrier' of the virus of new technology is not the foreign individual, but the foreign corporations."[22]

In more formal terms, using $A(t)$ to denote the total productivity of the factors in the advanced country, and assuming that

---

[21] Veblen (1915) and Gerschenkron (1962).

[22] Findlay (1978, p. 4).

it increases at a constant rate $n$, we have:

$$A(t) = A_0 e^{nt}. \tag{2.5}$$

Moreover, with $B(t)$ denoting the total productivity of the relatively more backward country, Veblen's and Gerschenkron's hypothesis can be represented as follows (the dot above a variable indicates its derivative with respect to time):

$$\dot{B} = \lambda [A_0 e^{nt} - B(t)], \tag{2.6}$$

where $\lambda$ is a positive constant dependent on exogenous parameters like the educational level of the relatively more backward country, the availability of productive infrastructures, and so on. Assuming that the relatively more advanced country is the one in which the FDI originates, and that the destination country is more backward, and also assuming that the foreign subsidiaries of MNEs make full use of the technology of their parent companies, Eq. (2.6) states the following: the wider the technological gap between MNEs and domestic firms, the greater convergence-type spillovers will be.

Using $GAP$ to indicate the technological gap between MNEs and domestic firms, and $FOR$ to indicate the degree of penetration by the former into the economy of the host country (Findlay considers the capital share owned by the MNEs), the convergence and contagion hypotheses can be represented as follows:

$$\dot{B}/B = f(GAP, FOR), \tag{2.7}$$

with

$$\frac{\partial f}{\partial GAP} > 0 \quad \text{and} \quad \frac{\partial f}{\partial FOR} > 0.$$

From Eqs. (2.5)–(2.7), with appropriate changes, one obtains the following relation:

$$\dot{GAP}/GAP = g(GAP, FOR), \tag{2.8}$$

with

$$\frac{\partial g}{\partial GAP} < 0 \quad \text{and} \quad \frac{\partial g}{\partial FOR} < 0,$$

which shows that catching-up by local firms will be the more rapid, the wider the technological gap and the greater the foreign presence.

Das (1987) uses a *game theory* approach to describe the interaction between a MNE and a 'fringe' of local firms, assuming, as in games *à la* Stackelberger, that the MNE (the leader) fixes the prices of its products once it is aware of those charged by local firms (the followers). Das bases his argument on the hypothesis that the MNEs enjoy oligopolistic advantages in the host countries — which give rise to a downward sloping demand curve — while domestic firms form a competitive fringe around them.

Das's model provides a much simpler description of technological spillovers than Findlay's. It considers, in fact, only contagion-type spillovers from process technologies. The rate of productivity growth in domestic firms is directly proportional to the output achieved in each period by the MNE, and every increase in the productive efficiency of the former group of firms reduces their average production costs.

Thus delineated, the game is resolved by the intertemporal maximisation of profits by the foreign firm, under the constraint that technological spillovers exist.

Das describes two possible scenarios. In the first, the technology of the foreign firm is given. Because local firms are able to learn, the foreign MNE's market shares and profits shrink, while the reverse process occurs in the fringe of local firms. Since the foreign firm is aware of this process, in order to counteract the decline in its profits, it maintains output at a level lower than it would in the absence of spillovers. In the second scenario, the foreign firm is able to import technology from its parent company, and thus manages to bolster its profit levels and market shares. Since output by the foreign firm is higher than in the previous scenario, the spillovers will be greater.

This latter conclusion is perhaps the most important implication of Das's model. The greater the amount of technology imported by foreign firms, the larger the spillovers will be. Since the transfer of technology from the parent company to its foreign subsidiaries becomes necessary because local firms learn foreign technologies, Das's model highlights the importance of interaction between domestic and foreign firms in determining the amount of technological spillovers.

Although Das did not conduct further analysis of this latter aspect, Wang and Blomstrom (1992) have constructed a model which develops the arguments of both Findlay and Das.

Wang and Blomstrom distinguish between 'contagion-type' and 'convergence-type' spillovers, on the one hand, and spillovers generated by competition between domestic firms and foreign MNEs ('competition-related' spillovers) on the other. As in Koizumi and Kopecky (1977), Findlay (1978) and Das (1987), contagion- and convergence-type spillovers are *automatically* triggered by the presence of foreign MNEs, and they are directly proportional to the technological gap between local firms and foreign subsidiaries. Competition-related spillovers, by contrast, are *endogenously* generated by the technological competition between foreign multinationals and domestic firms.

On the basis of results obtained by Teece (1977), Wang and Blomstrom assume that transferring technology among the various plants of a MNE is a costly process, and that the cost is directly proportional to the vintage of the technology transferred. Since the profitability of foreign subsidiaries depends on their technological superiority over local firms, when the latter exert only modest competitive pressure the foreign MNEs are not concerned to import new technologies. Consequently, in this case, "...*a large foreign presence may coexist with slow technology transfer and the transfer of 'old' technologies.*"[23]

Just as foreign firms must deploy resources for the transfer and adaptation of their proprietary technologies to the new environment, so the technological progress of domestic firms depends on the amount of resources that they devote to absorption of foreign technologies. The more resources utilised by local firms in order to learn foreign technologies, the greater will be the technological spillovers generated by the presence of foreign MNEs. Moreover, since learning by local firms tends to narrow the technological gap, a higher rate of investment by these firms will compel the subsidiaries of foreign multinationals to import

---

[23] Wang and Blomstrom (1992, p. 138).

new technologies in order to defend their market shares and to restore profitability to their investments, thereby increasing the amount of technological liable to spread to the surrounding environment.

Wang and Blomstrom's model can be outlined as follows. On the supply side, two firms, one domestic and the other a subsidiary of a foreign MNE, compete against each other by producing the same good using different technologies. On the demand side, consumers prefer technological advanced goods to relatively more mature ones. Their utility function is log-linear and is represented by the following equation:

$$U(Q) = \alpha \ln K_\text{d} + \ln(Q_\text{d} + k^\alpha Q_\text{f}) \quad \text{with } \alpha > 0, \qquad (2.9)$$

where the subscripts d and f respectively denote the domestic firm and the foreign subsidiary, $K$ stands for the level of technological development of each firm, $Q$ is the quantity produced and $k$ is the technological gap between the foreign and the domestic firm expressed by the ratio $K_\text{f}/K_\text{d}$.

Assuming that the price of every product is equal to its marginal utility, the partial derivatives of (2.9) with respect to $Q_\text{d}$ and $Q_\text{f}$ correspond to the demand functions of each firm:

$$P_\text{d} = (Q_\text{d} + k^\alpha Q_\text{f})^{-1} \quad \text{with } \partial P_\text{d}/\partial k < 0, \qquad (2.10)$$

$$P_\text{f} = k^\alpha (Q_\text{d} + k^\alpha Q_\text{f})^{-1} \quad \text{with } \partial P_\text{f}/\partial k > 0. \qquad (2.11)$$

In other words, the price charged by each firm depends on the quantity produced by each firm and on the appeal of each product as determined by its technological content. The wider the technological gap, the higher will be the price charged by the foreign firm or the quantity sold by it (or alternatively a combination of the two), and vice-versa for the domestic firm.

Competition among firms is represented by a Cournot game in which each firm decides the quantity to produce in order to maximise its profit, $R$, given output by the rival firm:

$$R_i(k) = \underset{Q_i}{MAX} \{ P_i(k_i, Q_i, Q_j) Q_i - c_i Q_i | Q_j \} \qquad (2.12)$$

where $c_i$ is the marginal (constant) cost of the $i$-th firm.

The technological progress achieved by the foreign subsidiary is directly correlated to the resources $I_f$ devoted to the importing of technology from the parent company:

$$\dot{K}_f = I_f K_f, \tag{2.13}$$

where, for the sake of simplicity, the marginal productivity of the technological investment is assumed equal to one.

As regards the domestic firm, the technological progress achieved in each period is assumed to be directly proportional to investments in learning activity, $I_d$, which is at decreasing returns. Moreover, incorporating Findlay's hypothesis on the 'advantages of backwardness', Wang and Blomstrom hypothesise that the rate of technical progress achieved by local firms will be inversely proportional to the technological gap:

$$\dot{K}_d = \phi(I_d) k K_d \quad \text{with } \phi' > 0, \ \phi'' < 0, \ \phi(0) = v > 0. \tag{2.14}$$

The difference between (2.13) and (2.14) represents the change over time in the technological gap between the two firms:

$$\dot{k} = [I_f - \phi(I_d) k] k. \tag{2.15}$$

Equations (2.10)–(2.15) show that the investment decisions of both firms jointly determine the amount of technological spillovers. First, each investment decision has a direct effect on the technological gap and consequently on the amount of convergence-type spillovers. Second, because the strategy of one firm influences the decisions of the other, competition-related spillovers are generated. Every change in the technological gap caused by the investment decisions of one of the two firms has a negative effect on demand for the product of the other. It consequently stimulates new investments by the rival and thus generates a virtuous circle of technological development.

Note that, compared with Findlay's model, Wang and Blomstrom's entirely lacks contagion-type spillovers, since there is no relation that ties technological spillovers to penetration by the foreign firm on the national territory. However, as Kokko (1992) has noted, since a wider technological gap implies a greater demand for the goods produced by the MNE (and therefore a larger market share) it is possible to establish a linkage between contagion-type spillovers and the technological gap on the basis of Eq. (2.14).

The solution of the model is obtained from the intertemporal maximisation of profits expressed by Eqs. (2.16) and (2.17):

$$V_f = \int_0^\infty e^{-rt} [R_f(k) - C_f(I_f)] \, dt, \qquad (2.16)$$

$$V_d = \int_0^\infty e^{-\rho t} [R_d(k) - \theta C_d(I_d)] \, dt, \qquad (2.17)$$

where $r$ and $\rho$ are the discount rates applied respectively by the MNE and the domestic firm, and $\theta$ is a parameter denoting the costs-side efficiency of the learning process undertaken by the domestic firm. The greater $\theta$ is, the greater the reduction in costs associated with a given expenditure $I_d$ on learning. Both Eqs. (2.16) and (2.17) may be maximised under the condition expressed by Eqs. (2.10) and (2.11). Resolving the two problems of intertemporal optimisation demonstrates the existence of a single Nash equilibrium, with which are associated two positive values of the variables $I_d$ and $I_f$. In steady state, the output of both firms, and their respective market shares, is stable over time, and so too is the technological gap between them.

## 2.6. TECHNOLOGICAL SPILLOVERS IN EMPIRICAL ANALYSIS

The empirical literature on technological spillovers is both scant and markedly heterogeneous. The lack of statistics on the activities of non-American multinationals has always hindered empirical verification of theoretical hypotheses. Those studies that do exist restrict themselves to a very small number of countries, and very often refer only to the 1960s and 1970s. The shortage of data is probably also responsible for the hetero-geneity of the empirical analyses available. While some studies employ cross-sector analysis, others concentrate on individual sectors, on groups of firms or even on individual firms. The majority of them examine intra-industry spillovers, while only a handful address the difficult topic of inter-industry spillovers.

These features of empirical analyse strongly affect their explanatory capacity. First of all, the fact that the bulk of statistical documentation dates back to at least two decades ago suggests that the relations they identify are very different from those that prevailing today. Secondly, since most of these analyses refer to developing countries, they are of only limited applicability to the industrialised ones. Moreover, analyses based on individual firms or groups of firms are likely to be strongly influenced by their choice of sample.

Leaving it to the reader to judge these matters in individual cases, in what follows I shall provide only a brief description of the techniques employed by various authors, the statistics utilised, and the main results obtained.

## Productivity and Foreign Penetration

The first analysis based on a cross-sector approach was a study by Caves (1974). Using data on twenty-two Australian industrial sectors in 1966, Caves showed that labour productivity in domestic industries was positively correlated with the degree of penetration by foreign MNEs in each production sector. Globerman (1979) reached the same conclusion on studying a sample of sixty Canadian manufacturing sectors in the same year. Similar results have been obtained by Blomstrom and Persson (1983) and by Kokko (1992), both with reference to 215 Mexican industries in 1970.

All these studies use a static approach. The average value added per employee in domestic firms is set against the degree of foreign participation in the national industry, measured as the percentages of the workforce or sales volume controlled by foreign MNEs in each sector, while a set of explanatory variables (capital/labour ratio, degree of concentration, quality of the workforce, etc.) are used to account for inter-sectoral differences in labour productivity not due to differing degrees of foreign penetration.

This approach suffers from a major shortcoming, however, which Blomstrom (1989) himself noted, as well as Aitken and Harrison (1991) and Globerman, Ries and Vertinsky (1994): namely that the higher productivity of domestic firms in sectors with greater foreign participation may derive from the tendency of MNEs to concentrate on industrial branches in which *ceteris paribus* (i.e. with the capital/labour ratio, degree

of concentration, and so forth, remaining equal) labour productivity is already higher.

This objection does not apply to the studies by Blomstrom
and Wolff (1989) and by Haddad and Harrison (1993), who
adopt a dynamic approach to technological spillovers, although
in this case possible distortions may arise from the tendency
of MNEs to concentrate on sectors characterised by above
average productivity growth.

With reference to the performance of Mexican firms in twenty
manufacturing sectors between 1970 and 1975, Blomstrom and
Wolff (1989) report that both the rate of productivity growth in
domestic firms and the latters' ability to catch up with the
subsidiaries of foreign MNEs are positively correlated with the
level of foreign penetration in the sector. However, the same
authors (Blomstrom and Wolff, 1993) note that, once account
has been taken of changes in the size of these firms between
1965 and 1975, the foreign presence exerts no significant influence on the rate of growth of labour productivity in Mexican
manufacturing industry. Similar conclusions have been reached
by Haddad and Harrison on the basis of single-firm data for
Moroccan manufacturing industry between 1980 and 1985.
They show that the presence of foreign MNEs did not significantly influence the growth of total factor productivity in
domestic firms.[24]

Of the studies cited above, that by Kokko (1992) warrants
further comment on account of the idiosyncrasy of its approach.
Kokko, in fact, divides his sample of industries into a number
of subsamples based on the technological gap between foreign
and domestic firms, on the capital/labour ratio, on the level of
foreign penetration, on the degree of market concentration, and
on technological complexity. He finds that in sectors with a
wide technological gap, a strong foreign presence, marked
technological complexity and a high capital/labour ratio,
domestic firms are substantially isolated from foreign MNEs,
and that there is no significant correlation between foreign
presence and the level of productivity of domestic firms.

Hence derives Kokko's hypothesis of the dualistic structure
of the Mexican economy, characterised by 'enclaves' in which
competition between multinational and domestic firms is
limited because they produce heterogeneous goods for different

---

[24] On the contrary, they report a partial negative, albeit not significant, correlation.

segments of the market. Typically, in fact, in a developing country like Mexico, industries with high technological complexity, strong market concentration or large economies of scale, and markedly differentiated demand, display a sharp separation between local firms, which use mainly labour-intensive technologies and produce goods for the lower segments of the market, and foreign firms characterised by more modern technologies, high capital intensity, and relatively sophisticated final demand in terms of the technological content of the goods demanded.[25]

Another way to analyse the effect of foreign presence on the technological capacity of domestic firms is to observe the relationship between foreign presence and deviations from best-practice technique within each production sector. Both Blomstrom (1986) and Haddad and Harrison (1993) address this problem.

Using the sample of Mexican companies described above, Blomstrom notes that the dispersion of labour productivity within each manufacturing sector is negatively correlated with the degree of foreign penetration. However, no significant relations emerge which tie the foreign presence to productivity growth either in the group of more efficient firms (i.e. to forward shifts in the technological frontier) or in the more backward ones (suggesting that the presence of foreign firms does not have significant displacement effects on less efficient local firms).[26]

---

[25] Kokko's results regarding the technological gap are ambiguous, however. As he himself acknowledges, although there is empirical evidence for the existence of a dualistic structure of the economy in sectors characterised simultaneously by a wide technological gap and strong market concentration, dividing the sample of industries on the basis of the technological gap in a cross-section analysis may give rise to considerable selection bias. Automatically allocated to the subsample of industrial sectors characterised by a wide technological gap, in fact, are precisely those sectors in which the gap at time $t$ is wide because of the lack of technological spillovers. See on this Kokko (1992, pp. 162–4).

[26] Because of a lack of data at the level of individual firms, Blomstrom examines productivity in various size classes comprising both domestic firms and foreign multinationals. This procedure raises three major problems. First, it is not possible to discriminate between technological spillovers and the direct effect exerted by the presence of MNEs on the dispersion of productivity within individual size classes. Second, the calculation of productivity at the level of the size class underestimates the dispersion of techniques. Third, the intertemporal comparison of productivity growth suffers from the fact that the sample of firms in each size class may change over time because of the passage of firms from one size class to another.

Largely the same results are obtained by Haddad and Harrison. The presence of MNEs encourages domestic firms to aggregate around the sector's production frontier. However, this effect is more marked in low-tech sectors than in high-tech ones, suggesting that the stimulus provided by competition from foreign firms tends to push firms towards the domestic technological frontier, rather than encourage the transfer of advanced technology, and/or that, in high-tech sectors, technological spillovers are impeded by the presence of an over-wide technological gap between local and foreign firms.

## Endogenous Spillovers

In the above survey of theoretical studies of technological spillovers, I emphasised the importance of externalities generated by technological competition between domestic firms and foreign multinationals resulting in the endogenously determined spillovers within the competitive process described by Wang and Blomstrom's (1992) model. The question is explicitly addressed by Kokko's analysis (1992) but it is also treated, more or less overtly, by less recent studies.

Caves (1974), for example, notes that a decisive factor in explanation of labour productivity in domestic firms is the labour productivity of the foreign subsidiaries competing with them for the same markets. He accordingly stresses the need to take account of existing interactions between the two groups of firms.

As discussed in detail above, Cantwell (1989) emphasises the importance of technological competition among firms from different countries waged by dint of their production activity and international trade, and focuses on technological and capital accumulation as driving force of virtuous or vicious circles of development. Unlike other authors, Cantwell concentrates on market shares and on the technological competence developed by domestic firms, rather than on the productivity of the factors.

In an extensive analysis of the impact of the activities of American multinationals in Europe between 1955 and 1982, Cantwell shows how the "lethargic" European firms were able to close the competitiveness gap with their American rivals by establishing their own productive and commercial networks in sectors where the latter had accumulated solid technological experience. By contrast, in industrial sectors where the European technological tradition was weaker, the market shares of European firms were noticeably reduced by the competition raised by the European subsidiaries of American multinationals.

Cantwell demonstrates the existence, in certain circumstances, of mutual advantages arising from international production able to generate virtuous circles of development for the firms of both countries. This happens when the firms of both countries have accumulated substantial bodies of technological experience which, thanks to their international productive networks, come into contact and generate virtuous processes of technological competition which enable them to achieve new technological targets.

On analysing the entire sample of 156 Mexican industrial sectors in 1970, Kokko (1992) finds no evidence that labour productivity in domestic and foreign firms is *simultaneously* determined. However, his analysis of subsamples of industries shows that the interaction between the two groups of firms is an important factor in explaining the labour productivity of domestic firms in the case of industrial sectors characterised by less than 50% foreign penetration and by a wide technological gap. And it is especially important for those characterised by both low foreign penetration and low spending on the purchase of licences and patents. Moreover, the labour productivity achieved by local firms positively influences the corresponding productivity level of foreign firms, as regards both the groups of 165 industries and sectors with low foreign penetration and a wide technological gap.

### Government Policies and Technological Spillovers

An interesting question — one that has already emerged in the foregoing discussion — concerns the impact of government policies on technological spillovers. Some of the empirical studies already illustrated address this question in relation to the impact of protectionist trade policies on the productive externalities generated by the presence of foreign firms on the national territory. Once again different conclusions are reached.

Blomstrom and Persson (1983) fail to find evidence for significant correlation between protectionist policies and the productivity of Mexican firms. Haddad and Harrison (1993) detect a negative correlation between the presence of trade barriers and the productive efficiency of Moroccan firms; but they find no significant relationship with trade policies as far as the rate of growth of total factor productivity is concerned. Balasubramanyam, Salisu and Sapsford (1996) analyse the effects of FDI on the rate of growth of per-capita income in 46 developing countries and report the negative impact of protectionist policies.

## Other Evidence

A final group of studies on the effects of the presence of foreign firms on the technological level of domestic firms is based on *ad hoc* surveys rather than on data collected by industrial censuses, as in the case of the cross-section analyses discussed above. This category of studies — the largest — comprises a wide and heterogeneous variety of research, ranging from studies based on questionnaires administered to almost all the foreign MNEs operating within the borders of a certain country, and perhaps including a certain number of vertically or horizontally connected domestic firms, through studies examining the consequences of the behaviour of the subsidiaries of MNEs of a particular country in one or more foreign countries, to analyses focusing on a small number of MNEs. Although not all these studies expressly set out to measure technological spillovers, they warrant mention in view of the further information that they provide.

I have on several occasions referred to the study by Dunning (1958). This was the first and one of the widest-ranging *ad hoc* surveys conducted on the effects and features of foreign presence. On the basis of a questionnaire sent to all the American multinationals operating in Great Britain (which at that time formed the overwhelming majority of foreign firms in the country), as well as a sample of local firms, Dunning depicted the relationships between foreign MNEs and British firms, highlighting the frequent collaborative relationships between them and the profound rootedness of the subsidiaries of American multinationals in British soil. The latter, in fact, were concerned to promote not only the technological development of the domestic firms in their production chain, also that of their local competitors, in order to encourage the positive externalities generated by a higher level of technological development in the surrounding environment. According to Dunning, the stimulus provided by the foreign presence did not exhaust itself in the exchange of technologies between local firms and foreign multinationals. It expressed its full potential in the competitive pressure exerted by the foreign presence, which induced the British firms to seize every available technological opportunity in order to keep up with their foreign competitors.

Further evidence of a positive relationship between foreign presence and technological progress in local industry is provided by a study carried out by Mansfield and Romeo (1980), who show that in around one-third of the cases[27] that they examined the transfer of new technologies to the foreign subsidiaries of American multinationals accelerated the adoption of similar technological innovations by domestic competitors, and that this effect was greater for process than for product technologies. This latter finding can be explained by the relatively greater importance attributed by the managers interviewed to the practice of reverse engineering in the diffusion of technology, compared with other possible access channels to foreign technologies. In fact, since this practice only requires possession of the product to imitate, and not the physical presence of the production plants of foreign plants in the vicinity of the imitator firm (apart from possible demonstration effects), in the case of product technologies the usual channels of international trade suffice for the diffusion of product technologies. Which is plainly a difficult route for process technologies to follow.

The importance of the presence of the subsidiaries of foreign MNEs in stimulating the international diffusion of technology also emerges from a number of sectoral studies. Among these Tilton (1971) and Lake (1979) examine the cases of the European semiconductors and pharmaceutical industries respectively, highlighting the active role played by the subsidiaries of American firms in the diffusion of technology.

As we saw in discussion of Dunning's (1958) study, the degree of integration between the subsidiaries of foreign MNEs and the local economy is a decisive factor in the occurrence of technological spillovers. And this is a finding confirmed, with particular regard to vertical linkages, by numerous other studies. Lall (1978), for example, when examining vertical

---

[27] This indicates a certain weakness in their results, since the transfer of technology among the plants of MNEs is therefore irrelevant to its spread to domestic firms in the remaining two-thirds of cases.

relationships upstream and downstream of the production plants of the affiliates of foreign MNEs, detects a "direct relation" whereby powerful stimuli to accelerate (or retard) economic growth may be created.[28] In another analysis, this time of the vertical relationships established with local firms by two foreign corporations (one wholly foreign-controlled, the other a joint venture) producing tractors in India, Lall (1980) reports that the foreign MNEs played an active role in transferring technologies to vertically linked local firms, both by direct participating in the capital of local suppliers and by granting licences on their patents and providing technical services. Likewise, empirical studies on Australia,[29] Argentina[30] and the Philippines[31] show that local suppliers to foreign MNEs are strongly stimulated to achieve the quality standards and machining times set by the production processes of foreign subsidiaries. But even more important in terms of the present discussion are the findings of Dunning (1986), who analyses the results of a questionnaire sent to the subsidiaries of Japanese firms operating in Great Britain and concludes:

> "The technical assistance given to their suppliers is often very considerable indeed. Besides providing detailed specifications, drawings, samples and prototypes, Japanese firms may, and do, give advice on plant layout, machinery, tooling, training of operatives, production methods, testing and quality control procedures; and help their suppliers to get in touch with their opposite numbers in Japan." (p. 112)

> "...there are some quite spectacular success stories of UK suppliers rising to the Japanese challenge, taking advantage of the advice given by customers, and building (or rebuilding) their business as a result." (p. 115)

Besides the importance of vertical connections, a number of studies have emphasised the crucial role played by the subsidiaries of foreign multinationals in the training of local labour and managers. Albeit with marked differences of emphasis,

---

[28] Lall also identifies an "indirect relation" operating through the changes in the industrial structure brought about by FDI. These changes have repercussions on the entire economic system through the causal relations described by the structure–behaviour–performance paradigm.

[29] Brash (1966).

[30] Katz (1969).

[31] Watanabe (1983).

Behrman and Wallender (1976), Chen (1983), Katz (1987) and Gerschenberg (1987) all agree on the importance of the mobility of human capital enhanced by employment in the subsidiaries of foreign multinationals for the industrialisation of developing countries.

All the studies discussed in this section extol the role of MNEs in driving the industrial development of the host countries. However, a number of points need making if the relevance of these studies to the present analysis is to be properly assessed. First, as in the case of the cross-sector inquiries of previous sections, the majority of these studies refer to situations historically (the 1950s and 1960s) and economically (the developing countries) distant from that of the more industrialised countries of today. Second, the methodology used — a questionnaire sent to the subsidiaries of foreign multinationals — may have considerably distorted the results, given that the respondents were obviously concerned to emphasise the positive role of foreign MNEs. Third, in the case of interviews with the managers of domestic firms vertically linked with foreign MNEs, positive effects may be counterbalanced by the harm caused to local firms excluded from the productive networks of foreign firms.

Furthermore, both cross-sector studies and those analysed in this sub-section find it difficult to distinguish between the impact exerted by the entry of foreign MNEs and the more general effects of ongoing competition in international markets. Since the sectors most affected by international production are those in which MNEs are induced by the competitiveness of their rivals to reduce costs and to improve the quality of their products by, amongst other things, transferring part of their production abroad — thereby profiting from the locational advantages offered by other countries — it may be that the stimulus received by local firms derives less from a certain degree of foreign penetration than, more generally, from strong competition on international markets.

## 2.7. CONCLUSIONS

The foregoing survey of the literature on the effects of the presence of foreign MNEs on the competitiveness of the host countries has evidenced the wide divergence of views on the subject and the lack of empirical study, especially as regards the current situation of the developed economies. The following chapters will explore both the theoretical and empirical aspects of this problem, focusing in particular on the phenomenon of FDI in the European countries.

Drawing on the arguments of previous sections in this chapter, I shall seek to distinguish — as far as possible — between the direct and indirect effects of FDI. In parallel, I shall further explore the dichotomy between productivity spillovers and technological spillovers, highlighting the differences between the productivity growth of local firms deriving from crowding-out effects and that which instead stems from the diffusion of technology.

Regarding the aspects of the problem which, although more theoretical are nevertheless crucial for correct specification of the empirical analysis, the next chapter is the natural continuation of this one. After outlining the principal features of the theoretical models discussed above, I shall examine the relationship between the presence of the subsidiaries of foreign MNEs and the technological and productive development of the domestic industrial system. I shall then present a new theoretical model which comprises both technology diffusion and the crowding-out of less competitive local firms.

As will become clear, development of these arguments will cast serious doubt on theoretical analyses of spillovers, as well as on most of the empirical contributions on the topic. It will be shown, in fact, that a possible positive association between foreign presence and the productivity of domestic firms may result, not from the healthy development of the competitive advantages of the national industrial base, but from the rapid displacement of local firms brought about by the strong competitive pressure generated by FDI.

Account will be taken of the results of this analysis in the following chapter devoted to empirical analysis. Chapter 4 is mainly concerned with the direct effects of the transfer of productive capital and technological knowledge by American and Japanese multinationals to European countries. Chapters 5 and 6 will analyse the indirect effects associated with the passive internationalisation of, respectively, the British and Italian industrial systems.

# 3. An Evolutionary Model of Technological Spillovers

## 3.1. INTRODUCTION

A main characteristic of the models of technological spillovers from foreign MNEs, which have been described in the preceding chapter is the existence of a positive relationship between foreign presence and spillovers. This conclusion evidently contrasts with a large part of the most recent literature, emphasising that the foreign presence may lead to both virtuous and vicious circles of development according to a number of factors which affect the ability of indigenous firms to successfully imitate foreign technologies.

In the model developed in this chapter I have tried to bridge the gap by including the indigenous firms' absorptive capacity, the level of the foreign penetration and the selective environment within an evolutionary model of technological spillovers from foreign MNEs.

## 3.2. FOREIGN PRESENCE, TECHNOLOGICAL GAP AND HOST COUNTRY'S TECHNOLOGICAL DEVELOPMENT

Before we pass to introduce the equations of the model is worth to spend some words about the theoretical schema below it. Figure 3.1 reproduce the three main forces responsible of the

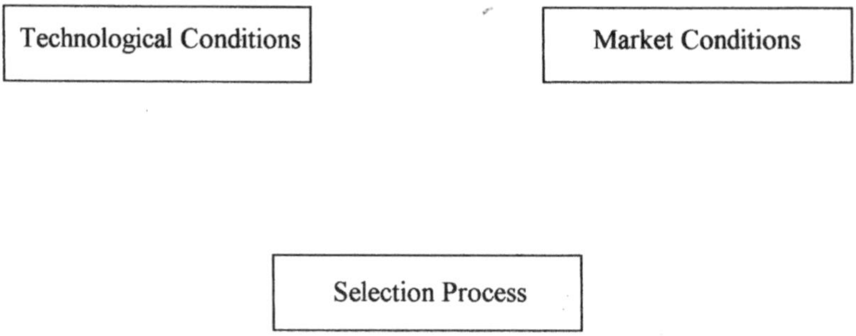

| Technological Conditions |

| Market Conditions |

| Selection Process |

**Figure 3.1**   Technological Conditions, Market Conditions and Selection Processes (1)

main dynamic of the model, namely, technological conditions, market conditions and market selectiveness.

The role of technological conditions in the process of imitation of foreign technologies has been widely described by several authors but using very different arguments. On the one, it has been put forward that the wider the distance between foreign and domestic firms the greater the opportunities for indigenous firms to achieve higher level of efficiency, according to the well-known "advantages of backwardness" hypothesis. This idea constituting the ground for the models briefly outlined in the preceding chapter. On the other hand, it has been asserted that a wide gap impairs indigenous firms ability to catch-up foreign competitors.

The model developed here heavily relies on this second strand of analysis. It rests in fact on the assumption that both the ability of firms to follow and to adapt to their needs technologies developed elsewhere and to pursue independent lines of technological development depends on their existing level of technological competence. An extensive argumentation for this assumption may be drawn both from the discussion of the preceding chapter and from a wide literature concerning the microeconomic firm level (Cohen and Levinthal, 1989), the industrial development (Kristensen, 1974; Rostow, 1980; Baumol, Blackman and Wolff, 1989; Verspagen, 1993) and the international business itself (Cantwell, 1989, 1993).

The second vertex of the schema in Figure 3.1 (market conditions) refers to the level and the pace of increase of the foreign presence. Again the analysis of this chapter divert substantially from the models of technological spillovers from foreign MNEs illustrated in Chapter 2. In fact, it is assumed that a given level of foreign presence might turn to be either beneficial or deleterious for the domestic industry depending on a number of circumstances that affects the ability of domestic firms to face competition by foreign MNEs. A relatively high level of foreign presence can be easily associated with the technological upgrading of the domestic industry when domestic firms are close to foreign competitors in terms of the degree of technological competence. Instead, when the distance between the two group of firms is wide, a much lower level of foreign presence may cause a severe reduction of domestic firms' profits, hence impairing their ability to raise resources for R&D investment and imitative learning. Similarly, a fast growing inward investment may displace indigenous firms, while a slower rate of foreign penetration might be compatible with increasing efforts by laggarding indigenous firms to catch up foreign competitors.

Such characteristic of the model fits nicely with some of the most recent analyses of the impact of inward FDI onto the technological and industrial development of domestic firms. Cantwell (1989), for instance, suggests that when domestic technological tradition is weak, the ability of foreign MNEs to rapidly increase their market penetration into the host economy, may force indigenous firms to cut back on research or to concentrate on narrower fields of specialisation. Porter (1990) put forward that "...*widespread foreign investment usually indicates that the process of competitive upgrading in an economy is not entirely healthy because domestic firms in many industries lack the capabilities to defend their market position against foreign firms.*"[1] Empirical evidence collected by Globerman and Meredith (1984) for Canada and by Veugelers and Vanden Houte (1990) for Belgium suggests that a foreign presence reduces indigenous firms' R&D expenditure, while Kokko (1992) does not detect any positive effect of foreign presence on the productivity level of Mexican firms in sectors characterised by a high (over 50%) foreign share and/or a wide technological gap. Moreover, the model developed by Wang and Blomstrom (1992), analysed in the preceding chapter relies on the hypothesis that spillovers do not arise 'automatically'

---

[1] Porter (1990, p. 671).

from foreign presence but instead required learning investment by domestic firms. Hence, since learning investment are
financed by a firm's profits, the dynamic of the model implies
that when the gap is wide, a high foreign presence erodes domestic firms' profits and learning investment.

The binomial technological disparities/foreign presence already contains most of the characteristic of the model illustrated in the following section. However, a further important
element of it is the presence of selective process within each
market. I suggest that market selection processes driven by
technological disparities may constitute the interface by which
technological and market conditions interact with one another.
A tight selective environment will imply a strong relationship
between a firm's competitiveness and its level of profits. Hence,
market selectiveness will ensure the survival of only few firms
very homogenous in terms of technological competence. *Vice
versa*, a loose selective environment will permit even firms that
lag far behind the technological frontier to earn sufficient
profits to finance the investment required in order not to fall
further behind competitors (Teece, Pisano and Shuen, 1990;
Cantwell, 1993).

The full picture of the dynamic of the model is depicted in
Figure 3.2. Technological and market conditions constitute the
inputs of the selective process in determining a firm's relative
competitiveness (which depends on each firm's market share
and absolute competitiveness, as it will be more formally set

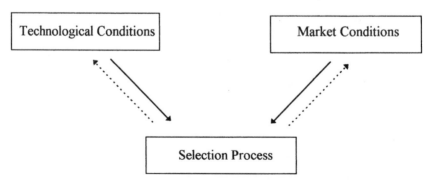

**Figure 3.2**  Technological Conditions, Market Conditions and Selection
Processes (2)

out in the following section) and its absorptive capacity. The
selection mechanism processes this information and sets the
resultant change in a firm's market share and its actual level of
profits. Consequently, the output of the selective process influences the technological and market conditions of the subsequent period by determining resources available for learning
investment, new machinery and capital equipment, each firm's
market share, and, hence, each firm's productivity growth and
relative competitiveness.

Clearly, additional circumstances might alter or reinforce
the causation mechanism at work by affecting one or more
elements of this stylised representation. For instance, the
growth of demand associated with new FDI and average
productivity growth might partly offset the tightness of the
selective environment. Government intervention by financing
R&D expenditure, favouring technological co-operation between foreign and indigenous firms and/or regulating FDI
flows can alter the competitive game and the spread of the
leaking out of technological knowledge from foreign plants.

## 3.3. THE MODEL

The preceding section has been dedicated to a presentation of
the principal factors affecting the interrelationship between
FDI and the technological development of indigenous firms.
Accordingly, the following pages will be devoted to developing
a model that embodies the following properties:

(i)   technological spillovers depend on the absorptive capacity
      of firms;
(ii)  technology imports by foreign firms are inversely related to
      the existing technological gap;
(iii) a firm's market share dynamic depends on its technological
      level relative to the other firms operating in the market;
(iv)  the dimension of the market grows with the national
      income according to a Keynesian-type demand formation
      mechanism.

Some possible extensions of the model will be discussed in the
final part of this section.

In formulation of the model, I have drawn extensively on the work by Dosi and Freeman (1992) aimed at explaining the process of forging ahead and falling behind among countries according to an evolutionary perspective.[2] However, substantial changes have been made with respect to the original formulation. Firstly, given the scope of this paper, equations describing the interaction between foreign MNEs and indigenous firms at the technological level have been incorporated into the model. This has been done to take account of some of the more interesting lines of development in the recent literature concerning technological spillovers from foreign MNEs. As in the Wang and Blomstrom (1992) model, the decision by foreign firms to import new technology depends on the existing technological gap between foreign and indigenous firms, while the imitation of foreign technology requires specific investment. Secondly, for the sake of simplicity, the number of parameters has been reduced by eliminating stochastic processes and foreign trade. Thirdly, the model refers to a single-sector economy.

Although comprising these substantial modifications with respect to Dosi and Freeman's work, the model illustrated below still belongs within the realm of evolutionary economics. In fact, it displays two of the main characteristics of that tradition. The first is the existence of a strong path-dependency: the absorptive capacity of indigenous firms depends on their past process of technological accumulation, this being a major cause of virtuous or vicious circles of technological development. Secondly, heterogeneity among individuals (e.g., between foreign and domestic enterprises or within each group of firms) is explicitly recognised as a cause of evolutionary paths, driven by market selectiveness.[3]

The version of the model presented in the following pages represents an extension of an earlier model which I developed in Perez (1997). In the new formulation domestic firms are allowed to devote resources both in imitative and searching

---

[2] See also Dosi and Fabiani (1994).

[3] Conversely, a third characteristic of the evolutionary approach, namely its probabilistic nature, is not present in my model, so as not to complicate my formulation and numeric simulations with elements that do not affect significantly the issues analysed. However, probabilistic processes may be easily re-introduced without changing the main framework of the model.

activities. The amount of resources which are allocated in the two activities depends on the existing level of technological disparities between foreign and indigenous firms. When the technology disparities are in favour of foreign firms a relatively greater part of resources is devoted to imitative activities than when domestic firms are ahead of foreign rivals. With respect to imitative activities, searching activities show a lower impact on labour productivity growth due to the greater difficulties of searching with respect to imitation.

For what concerns the behaviour of foreign firms, I make FDI endogenously determined within the model. The lower are the real wages paid by foreign firms, the higher FDI flows will be.

## Market Selection Process

Following Silverberg, Dosi and Orsenigo (1988), it is assumed that the evolution of the market share of indigenous firms in terms of total output ( $f$ ) depends on their relative competitiveness ($RC$) *vis-à-vis* the other firms operating in the market (the symbol $\dot{f}(t-1,t)$ stands for the change occurred in the value of $f$ between $t-1$ and $t$):

$$\dot{f}_i(t-1,t) = \alpha[RC_i(t-1)-1]f_i(t-1).$$

Taking into account that $f_i(t) = Q_i(t)/Q(t)$, where $Q_i$ and $Q$ are a firm's and total output, and assuming, for the sake of simplicity, the existence of only two firms — one domestic (firm 1) and one foreign (firm 2) representative of the two group of firms[4] — the previous equation has been reformulated as regards the domestic firm into:

$$\dot{Q}_1(t-1,t) = \alpha[RC_1(t-1)-1]\frac{Q_1(t-1)}{Q(t-1)}Q(t)$$

$$+ \frac{Q_1(t-1)}{Q(t-1)}\dot{Q}(t-1,t), \qquad (3.1)$$

---

[4] This assumption will be removed later in this section.

with

$$RC_i(t) = \frac{E_i(t)}{\bar{E}(t)}, \tag{3.2}$$

$$E_i(t) = \frac{1}{P_i(t)}, \tag{3.3}$$

$$\bar{E}(t) = \sum_i f_i(t) E_i(t), \tag{3.4}$$

where $P_i$ is the price charged by the $i$-th firm and $E_i$ its absolute competitiveness.

Similarly, the output dynamic of the foreign firm depends on its relative competitiveness and on the flows of new foreign direct investment (FDI), measured in terms of the additional investment available to employ new workers ($N^{\text{FDI}}$):

$$\dot{Q}_2(t-1,t) = \alpha[RC_2(t-1)-1]\frac{Q_2(t-1)}{Q(t-1)}Q(t)$$
$$+ \frac{Q_2(t-1)}{Q(t-1)}\dot{Q}(t-1,t) + N^{\text{FDI}}(t)\pi_2(t)P_2(t),$$

$$\tag{3.5}$$

with

$$N^{\text{FDI}}(\tau) = \frac{FDI(t)}{w_2(t)}, \tag{3.6}$$

where FDI flows are inversely dependent upon real wages paid by foreign firms,

$$FDI(t) = \tau \cdot \exp\left(-\frac{w_2}{p_2}\right). \tag{3.7}$$

Each firm fixes prices according to a simple mark-up rule over labour costs:

$$P_i(\tau) = (1+\rho)\frac{w_i(t)}{\pi_i(t)}, \tag{3.8}$$

where $w$ is the nominal wage, $\pi_i$ the real labour productivity and $\rho$ the mark-up.

Workers use all the wages received at time $t-1$ to buy goods in the following period. Thus, total demand, which is equal to total output, as we shall see later, is equal to:

$$Q(t) = \sum_i [w_i(t-1)N_i^P(t-1) + w_i(t-1)N_i^{IMI}(t-1)]$$

$$+ w_1 N^{SEARCH}(t-1) + w_2 N^{FDI}(t-1), \tag{3.9}$$

where $N^P$, $N^{IMI}$ and $N^{SEARCH}$ are the number of workers engaged in, respectively, productive, imitating and searching activities.

### Technology Import, Imitation and Searching

As has been discussed above, it is assumed that a firm's productivity growth depends:

(a) on its capability to imitate other firms' technology;
(b) on resources that it devotes to learning and imitative activities, or in the case of foreign firms on technology imports.

Thus, the indigenous firm's labour productivity growth is related to the technological gap *vis-à-vis* the foreign MNE (proxy for domestic firm's level of technological competence), which is defined as the ratio between labour productivity in foreign and domestic plants (i.e., $GAP(t) = \pi_2(t)/\pi_1(t)$), and to the number of workers engaged in the learning activity and searching activities. As the productivity gap increases, spillovers also increase up to a certain critical level of it: thereafter absorptive capacity declines.

$$\frac{\dot{\pi}_i(t-1,t)}{\pi_i(t-1)} = \mu_1 + \lambda_0[1 - \exp\{-\eta_1 N_1^{IMI}(t-1)\}]$$

$$\times \frac{GAP(t-1)}{\exp\{\lambda_1 GAP(t-1)\}}$$

$$+ \lambda_2(1 - \exp(-\eta_2 N^{SEARCH})). \tag{3.10}$$

In the numerical simulations reported below, parameter $\lambda_1$ has been set equal to 1. Therefore, the maximum of the function lies at the point where the distance between foreign and domestic firms is equal to its minimum value (i.e., where $GAP = 1$), as suggested by John Cantwell's approach to technological competition. Lower values of the parameter would instead be more close to the catching-up approach.

As regards the foreign firm, it is assumed that productivity growth depends on two different factors: (i) the decision to import new technologies from its mother company and (ii) the imitation of domestic firms' technologies. For what concerns the technology import decision, it has been simply assumed that technology import is inversely related to the existing productivity gap between foreign and domestic firms. As concerns point (ii), technological spillovers from indigenous to foreign firms generate alike spillovers from foreign to indigenous enterprises. They are maximised for small gaps and decrease as the gap move away in both directions.[5]

$$\frac{\dot{\pi}_2(t-1,t)}{\pi_2(t-1)} = \mu_2 + \delta_0[1 - \exp\{-\eta_1 N_2^{\mathrm{IMI}}(t-1)\}]$$

$$\times \frac{[1/GAP(t-1)]}{\exp\{\delta_1[1/GAP(t-1)]\}}$$

$$+ \delta_2 \exp\{-GAP(t-1)\}. \tag{3.11}$$

### Labour Market Dynamic

The last part of the model describes labour market dynamics. All profits are reinvested by firms in RD activities:

$$RD_i(t) = P_i(t)Q_i(t) - w_i(t)N_i^{\mathrm{P}}(t). \tag{3.12}$$

In the case of domestic firms a proportion $\theta$ of R&D expenditure is devoted to hire workers for imitating activities,

---

[5] The formulation of Eq. (3.11) has given rise to many problems. In fact, in the case of foreign firms it is difficult to identify an upper limit of resources that can be devoted to technology import and imitation. In some circumstances, it is possible that such resources would be higher than profits, because of the easier access to capital with respect to domestic counterparts and/or because international sourcing strategies by MNEs might suggest the need to tap into foreign lines of technological development independently from the profitability of the foreign subsidiary. However, it should be noted that, if either the second or the third element of the rhs of Eq. (3.12) are eliminated, the dynamics of the model do not substantially change.

the remaining fraction goes to searching activities. The wider the technological disparities, the more the scope for imitation, hence, the higher is $\theta$:

$$\theta = [(1 - \exp(-GAP))], \tag{3.13}$$

$$N_1^{IMI} = \theta \, \frac{RD_1(t)}{w_1(t)}, \tag{3.14}$$

$$N_1^{SEARCH} = (1 - \theta) \frac{RD_1(t)}{w_1(t)}. \tag{3.15}$$

As concerns foreign firm, $\theta$ is supposed to be equal to 1, hence all R&D resources are devoted to imitative active.

As regards workers employed in the productive activity, firms instantaneously adjust employment to the level of demand:

$$N_i^P(t) = \frac{Q_i(t)}{P_i(t)\pi_i(t)}. \tag{3.16}$$

Nominal wages change with inflation, average productivity growth and total employment:

$$\frac{\dot{w}_i(t-1,t)}{w_i(t)} = \vartheta_1 \frac{\dot{\bar{\pi}}(t-2,t-1)}{\bar{\pi}(t-2)} + \vartheta_2 \frac{\dot{\bar{P}}(t-2,t-1)}{\bar{P}(t-2)}$$

$$+ \vartheta_3 \frac{\dot{N}(t-2,t-1)}{N(t-2)}, \tag{3.17}$$

with

$$\bar{\pi} = \sum_i f_i \pi_i, \tag{3.18}$$

$$\bar{P} = \sum_i f_i P_i, \tag{3.19}$$

$$N = \sum_i N_i^P + \sum_i N_i^{IMI} + N_1^{SEARCH} + N_2^{FDI}. \tag{3.20}$$

In the numerical simulations set out below, it is hypothesised that the wage dynamic is the same for both firms, but that wages paid by foreign firms are equal to $w_2(t)=(1+\varepsilon)w_1(t)$ with $\varepsilon>0$, in order to take into account the additional costs that foreign firms have to sustain to penetrate the host country's market.

## Simulation Results

In the numerical simulations reported, parameters were set up as follows: $\alpha=0.1$ (relatively weak market selection process), $\lambda_0=0.1$, $\lambda_1=1$, $\lambda_2=0.01$, $\eta_1=0.1$, $\eta_2=1$, $\delta_0=0.1$, $\delta_1=1$, $\delta_2=0.1$, $\mu_1=\mu_2=0$, $\vartheta_1=1$, $\vartheta_2=1$ (wages adjust completely to productivity and price growth), $\vartheta_3=1$, $\varepsilon=0.1$ (foreign firms face labour costs 10% higher than domestic firms), $\rho=0.1$ (mark up is 10% over production costs), $\tau=0.01$. The results reported refer to 30 iterations given the initial conditions $f_1=99\%$ and $f_2=1\%$.

A first group of simulations describes the dynamic of productivity gap and foreign penetration for different level of initial technological disparities between foreign and domestic firms. The results obtained highlight the influence of the initial technological gap on the 'success' or the 'failure' of domestic firms faced with foreign competition. Three different types of reaction emerge.

When the initial technological gap is wide, domestic firms do not have the necessary absorptive capacity to imitate successfully foreign technology (Figure 3.3). The market selection process drives indigenous competitors out of the market, eroding domestic firms' profitability and, hence, their investment in learning. Foreign firms permeate the economy. Moreover, since indigenous firms exert a very moderate competitive pressure over foreign firms, technology import is modest and the location concerned becomes the basis for low value-added activities by foreign MNEs.

Conversely, when the initial technological competence of domestic firms is high, they are able to reduce the original gap (Figure 3.4) and to contrast successfully competition from foreign firms, while the location attracts high-tech foreign MNE productive activities. Technological competition and spillovers interact with one another in a virtuous circle of technological development.

Of particular interest is an intermediate case characterised by an initial apparent process of catching up by domestic firms,

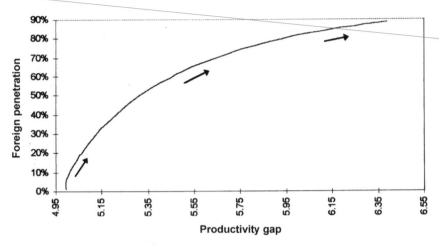

**Figure 3.3**  Simulation Results (1)

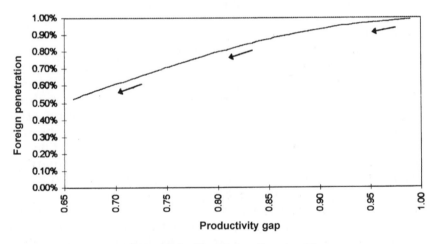

**Figure 3.4**  Simulation Results (2)

which subsequently changes into a rapid process of falling behind (Figure 3.5). In this case, the initial conditions in terms of technological gap and foreign penetration ensure sufficient profits for domestic firms to finance R&D activities for the successful imitation of foreign technologies. However, as the

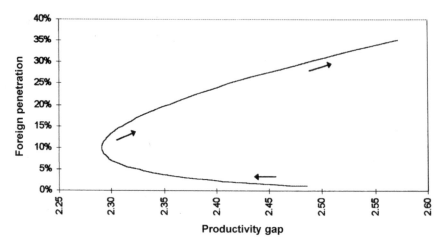

**Figure 3.5**   Simulation Results (3)

foreign presence increases, market conditions erode the domestic firms' profitability, causing the cumulative decline of the national industry.

A second set of simulations was performed in order to detect the relationship between initial technological disparities and the dynamic of productivity, employment and real output. Figures 3.6–3.8 depict the influence of initial disparities onto these three variables. At the productivity level positive interaction between foreign and indigenous firms are maximised when both groups of firms are at comparable level of initial technological development (Figure 3.6). Spillovers tend to wipe out as disparities become large. A further point to be noted in Figure 3.6 is the relationship between initial technological gap and average productivity growth. The latter is maximised for small and large gaps. Such a behaviour is the result of the interaction between technological spillovers and market selections processes. When the gap is narrow high rates of average productivity growth are driven by technological spillovers between foreign and domestic firms. When the gap is large, comparable rates of average productivity growth are due to the faster elimination of the less efficient enterprises (in our case domestic firms) driven by market selectiveness.

For what concerns total employment, when foreign and indigenous firms are close to the technological frontiers the positive

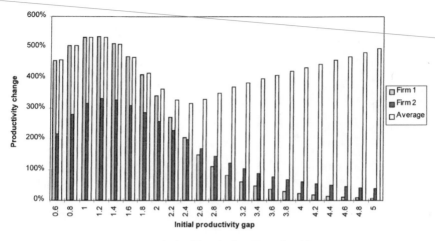

**Figure 3.6** Simulation Results (4)

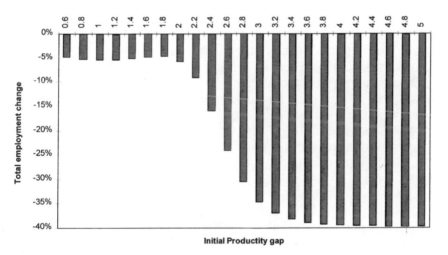

**Figure 3.7** Simulation Results (5)

effects that the interactions between the two groups of firms produces onto the growth of the domestic economy almost offsets the labour saving effects produced by productivity growth. *Vice versa*, as the gap increases competition by foreign firms cause a severe reduction of employment (Figure 3.7).

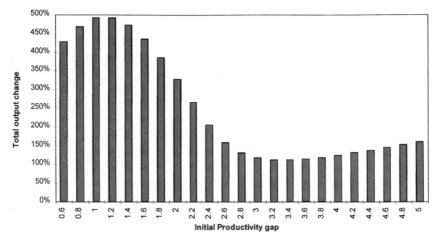

**Figure 3.8**   Simulation Results (6)

Similar effects arise with respect to real output growth. In this case as in the previous ones positive effects are maximised when foreign and indigenous firms are at the same level of development. However, as the gap increase the positive effects of the foreign presence on the real output tend first to decrease and then to increase again (Figure 3.8). Very low developed locations seem to benefit from FDI more than medium developed ones resembling John Cantwell's idea discussed in the previous chapter of a J-shaped relation between inward FDI and beneficial effects onto the host economy.[6]

### 3.4. CONCLUDING REMARKS AND POLICY IMPLICATION

The model developed here suggests that the effect of foreign MNE presence on the technological development of indigenous firms is likely to vary according to a number of circumstances. In particular, I have focused attention on three factors affecting the sign of the impact of in-flowing FDI on domestic firms'

---

[6] It is worth to recall that such a kind of relationship was much more pronounced in the first version of the model (Perez, 1997) where it interested also the productivity and real wage effects. Such a behaviour seems to crucially depend on the process which regulates productivity growth by domestic firms (Eq. (3.10)).

competitiveness, namely, the original technological gap between foreign and domestic firms, the level and the pace of increase of foreign presence, and the market selectiveness. In this respect, a large technological gap may impair the capacity of domestic firms to absorb foreign technology, while a foreign presence in rapid expansion might dramatically reduce their profitability and hence their investment in R&D, new machinery and capital equipment. A tight selective environment jeopardises the ability of laggarding indigenous firms to raise resources to upgrade their technological competitiveness.

On the basis of a theoretical model that adopts an evolutionary perspective, I have argued that when domestic firms excel in the development of a particular technology, they benefit from in-coming FDI. In this case, technological competition between foreign and domestic firms creates room for a large amount of technological spillovers. By the rapid absorption of foreign technologies, indigenous firms reduce the original gap and spur foreign MNEs to import more advanced technology. Conversely, indigenous firms lagging far behind foreign competitors are penalised by in-flowing FDI. The greater competitive pressure generated by the foreign presence erodes their profits and hence reduces their investment in learning activities, new machinery and capital equipment. This gives rise to a cumulative process of technological decline in the locations concerned, which eventually leads to a large presence of foreign firms specialised in low-tech productions.

The theoretical and the empirical analyses of the preceding pages challenge the *laissez-faire* view about in-flowing FDI as the optimal policy prescription. Instead, it is suggested that the positive (or negative) effects of the foreign MNE entry might be enhanced (offset) by regulating FDI flows and by taking actions to speed up the dissemination of foreign technologies among domestic firms, either by encouraging technological co-operation between foreign and indigenous enterprises or by financing R&D efforts by indigenous firms.

In the following chapters analysis will be devoted to illustrate how such a conclusion is confirmed by empirical analysis. Chapter 4 will investigate onto the characteristics of US and Japanese MNEs operations in Europe. Chapters 5 and 6 will examine the impact of the foreign presence onto British and Italian manufacturing firms. As we will see in both case significant relationships between technological disparities and domestic firms' reaction to foreign presence emerge.

# 4. Japanese and American Multinational Firms in Europe: Empirical Evidence for the 1980s and Early 1990s

## 4.1. INTRODUCTION

The scant and heterogeneous data on the activities of multinational firms in the European countries do not permit systematic analysis of the impact of the foreign presence on the competitiveness of countries receiving FDI. However, one important aspect of this broader phenomenon can be analysed using empirical evidence on the transfer and creation of productive and technological activities by MNEs.

More specifically, the analysis conducted in this chapter will concentrate on the behaviour and role of MNEs in the redistribution of innovative and productive activities among the countries of Western Europe in the 1980s and early 1990s. The aim will be to delineate the future patterns of national specialisation within the European Union generated by FDI.

After addressing a number of still unresolved questions concerning the effects of the redistribution of innovative activities among countries (Section 4.2), discussion will focus on the empirical evidence concerning the productive and innovative activities of the MNEs of all countries in the European nations (Section 4.3). Subsequently, the more abundant empirical data on the American and Japanese MNEs will be used to analyse the behaviour of these firms (Sections 4.4 and 4.5). Some conclusions are drawn in the final section.

73

## 4.2. THE INTERNATIONALISATION OF INNOVATIVE ACTIVITIES: POSSIBLE CONSEQUENCES FOR THE DESTINATION COUNTRIES

Since the second half of the 1980s economists have paid increasingly closer attention to the redistribution of innovative capabilities and technological knowledge among the industrialised countries brought about by the MNEs. There are various reasons for this interest, not least the clearer understanding of the process of creation and diffusion of technology yielded by years of study on the economics of technological innovation. Added to this is the greater concern of governments and economists with the implications of the growth of international production simultaneously with the decline in the rate of productivity growth of the leading Western countries, and with high rates of unemployment in these same countries. Within this scenario, the internationalisation of production is viewed either with alarm, because of its possible erosion of a country's scientific, technological and productive base, or as an important channel for the diffusion of foreign technologies from the technologically most advanced countries, principally Japan, and as a further stimulus to industrial development.

Leaving problems to do with international movements of productive capital aside for the moment, and concentrating on the technological activities of the MNEs, it should be noted that from the point of view of the recipient country, the location of R&D activities on the national territory, or the importing of technology by the subsidiaries of foreign MNEs, may give rise to diverse and often conflicting effects, which make it difficult to conduct direct comparison of the costs and benefits of this type of activity. Dunning (1992, 1994a) divides these possible consequences into *direct* and *indirect effects*. The former correspond to the increased innovative capacity of the host country resulting from the creation of new scientific and technological infrastructures, and from the transfer of the human capital and scientific knowledge necessary to utilise them. This advantage is off-set by the possible depressive effect of FDI on domestic technological capacity resulting either from the purchase of local firms with their own R&D facilities or from the displacement of actual or potential domestic competitors. Indeed, as discussed in Chapter 3, if the competition raised by the foreign MNEs reduces spending on R&D in local firms, the direct

effects may be generally negative rather than positive. Turning
to indirect effects, these principally concern the technological
spillovers that may result from FDI in general, or from the
international transfer of technological skills and knowledge
in particular. Concerning this latter aspect, on the one hand
the location of R&D activities in the destination country and the
importing of advanced technology has a positive effect on the
amount of technology liable to diffuse into the surrounding
environment and on stimuli to local firms to increase their
innovative effort in response to increased competitive pressure.
On the other hand, the greater competitiveness of the subsidiaries of foreign MNEs that results from the importing of
technology and/or the independent development of technological innovations by the subsidiaries may heighten the displacement effects on the national technological and productive base.

Assessment of the role played by the redistribution of technological knowledge and capacity involves the concept of the
*international competitiveness* or *competitive advantages* of a
country. Even if we assume that the transfer of technology or
infrastructures for the production of technological innovations,
like R&D laboratories, results in a net increase in a country's
technological and scientific assets (i.e. assuming that the net
balance of direct effects is positive), the question arises as to the
ownership of these assets. In other words, unless the firm
undertaking the transfer of technologies and technological skills
miscalculates, the operation will primarily increase the competitiveness of the multinational firm itself, with no direct effects
on a country's *national* technological assets and innovative capacity (i.e. belonging to resident firms or institutions). Indeed,
negative effects may arise because of the *draining* of the country's
more skilled human resources by foreign firms. The problem
therefore arises of calculating what proportion of this scientific
and technological capital can be definitively appropriated by the
host country. Assessment of this proportion is fraught with
difficulty, since the degree of appropriability is determined by a
large number of often unpredictable factors, such as the revers-
ibility of foreign investments (that is, the period of time that a
given type of investment lasts before its withdrawal or before
its significant quantitative or qualitative restructuring), the
amount and nature of technological spillovers, the displacement
effects on national industry deriving not only from the market
shares acquired by the subsidiaries of foreign multinational

firms in the host country (minus the previous imports replaced by local production) but also from the effects indirectly produced by the increased competitiveness of the foreign multinational group as a whole, and from consequent variations in the domestic firms' shares of international markets.[1]

Whatever the overall long-term effect may be, the majority of governments and economists pass positive judgement on FDI in activities with high value added and high scientific and technological content — especially if these are greenfield investments and not purchases of important national industries — rather than in activities with low value added and low scientific and technological content. This is because, firstly, high-tech activities generate greater direct benefits in terms of commercial performance, and possibly more significant technological spillovers, and secondly because encouraging incoming FDI in low-tech productions may relegate the domestic industrial system to a position of technological inferiority with respect to its principal international competitors, engendering possible lock-in on a path of economic development based on low labour costs and the abundance of unskilled labour. These risks are particularly high in an integrated supranational market like the European Union, internally to which the MNEs can easily redistributive the various phases of a productive chain among several countries according to the locational advantages that they offer in terms of labour costs or technological skills.

## 4.3. THE PRODUCTIVE AND INNOVATIVE ACTIVITY OF MULTINATIONAL FIRMS IN THE EUROPEAN COUNTRIES

During the 1980s, foreign penetration in terms of employment increased in many European countries and in the United States.

---

[1] An example of this phenomenon might be a Japanese car firm which installs an assembly plant in Great Britain in order to circumvent the restrictions on car imports imposed by the European Union. If the size of the market in Europe is given, British companies will not only suffer a fall-off in their sales in Britain but also a reduction of their market shares in the other European countries. Furthermore, if the subsidiary of the Japanese car company then imports most of its components from other firms in the group, rather than purchase them from local producers, the international competitiveness of a whole series of the group's activities connected with the assembly phase will be reinforced, with the consequent weakening of analogous production in Great Britain.

The only exceptions among the twelve countries listed in Figure 4.1 were Germany, Japan and Italy, which displayed a slight decrease in their shares of employees working for the subsidiaries of foreign multinational firms; a figure which in the case of Japan was already low.

As shown by Figure 4.1, FDI was quite uniformly distributed among the European countries, with the sole exception of Ireland (and probably of other small countries not listed due to the lack of data), where the foreign presence was well above the European average. However, differences in data-gathering methods counsel caution when conducting comparison among countries.

Aggregate figures such as these, however, tell us very little about the type of activity undertaken by the foreign subsidiaries of foreign MNEs in the various countries concerned, or about its technological content. Indicators of technological inputs and outputs provide clearer information on these matters.

Regarding the former of these two indicators (inputs), the subsidiaries of foreign firms accounted for a significant share of

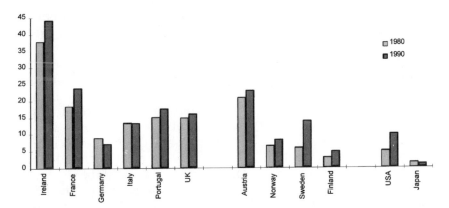

**Figure 4.1** Foreign Penetration in Terms of Employees, 1980 and 1990 (or Closest Available Year), Percentage Values
*Notes*: Ireland 1983 and 1988, Italy 1981 and 1984, Portugal 1981 and 1984, Great Britain 1981 and 1990, Norway 1980 and 1989, USA 1980 and 1989. The figures for France and the USA also include minority shareholdings (shareholdings amounting to more than 10% or 20% and less than 50% of share capital).
*Source*: My calculations on data from OECD, *Industrial Activity of Foreign Affiliates Data Bank*.

R&D in countries for which figures are available. In 1985, the percentage was 10.9% in Great Britain, 7.4% in France, and 6.5% in Italy (Stoneman, 1989). OECD sources indicate that in 1989 the figure was around 15% in France, Great Britain and Sweden. Even more important was the role played by foreign multinational firms in terms of technological output. Patel and Pavitt (1991) calculate that the foreign affiliates of the 686 largest firms in the world were responsible for 39.7% of the patents issued in the USA by firms resident in Belgium, 19.1% in Great Britain, and around 10% in France, Germany, Italy and Holland.

Again with reference to patents in the USA, Patel (1995) reports, on the basis of a sample restricted to the 569 largest firms, that the bulk of their technological activity takes place in the countries of origin (Table 4.1). The degree of internationalisation of innovative activity varies considerably according to the nationality of the firm. Japanese and American firms are those that tend most to concentrate their innovative activities in the home country, followed by Italian, French and German firms. The firms of smaller countries like Belgium, Holland and Switzerland instead display a high degree of internationalisation in their innovative activity, immediately followed by Great Britain.

Apart from Great Britain and Germany, all the other European countries prefer the other European countries as sites for their innovative activity abroad. Apparently none of them is able to exploit, except to an absolutely marginal extent, Japanese lines of technological development.

The first impression to be gained from these figures is that the technological content of activities by multinational firms is — at least on the basis of the data on patents — closely dependent on the nationality of the investor country. The firms of the leader countries in terms of technological development — the USA and Japan, which are also the countries from which the bulk of direct foreign investments originate — are those that display the least propensity to internationalise their innovative systems. Among the European countries, by contrast, geographical and cultural proximity, as well as economic integration, seem to have prompted the birth of an integrated (though yet largely to be developed) transnational innovative system which also draws impetus from its significant presence in American industry, as well as in the industries of other European countries.

Table 4.1   The Geographical Location of Patents Issued in the USA by the Largest Firms Worldwide, According to Nationality, 1985–1990

| Nationality of the Firm | Within the Country | Abroad | Of which: USA | Europe | Japan | Other Countries |
|---|---|---|---|---|---|---|
| Japan (139) | 99.0 | 1.0 | 0.8 | 0.2 | — | 0.0 |
| USA (243) | 92.2 | 7.8 | — | 6.0 | 0.5 | 1.3 |
| Italy (7) | 88.2 | 11.8 | 5.3 | 6.2 | 0.0 | 0.3 |
| France (25) | 85.7 | 14.3 | 4.8 | 8.7 | 0.3 | 0.6 |
| Germany (42) | 85.1 | 14.9 | 10.4 | 3.9 | 0.2 | 0.4 |
| Finland (7) | 82.0 | 18.0 | 1.6 | 11.5 | 0.0 | 4.9 |
| Norway (3) | 67.9 | 32.1 | 12.7 | 19.4 | 0.0 | 0.0 |
| Canada (16) | 67.0 | 33.0 | 24.9 | 7.3 | 0.3 | 0.5 |
| Sweden (13) | 60.8 | 39.2 | 12.6 | 25.6 | 0.2 | 0.8 |
| UK (54) | 57.9 | 42.1 | 31.9 | 7.1 | 0.2 | 3.0 |
| Switzerland (8) | 53.3 | 46.7 | 19.6 | 26.0 | 0.6 | 0.5 |
| Holland (8) | 42.2 | 57.8 | 26.1 | 30.6 | 0.5 | 0.6 |
| Belgium (4) | 37.2 | 62.8 | 22.2 | 39.9 | 0.0 | 0.6 |
| Total (569) | 89.1 | 10.9 | 4.1 | 5.6 | 0.3 | 0.8 |

*Notes*: The numbers in brackets in the first column indicate the number of companies with their headquarters in each of the countries. The other columns give the percentage of patents in the USA registered by the largest firms of each country in relation to the country in which application for the patent was made.
*Source*: Patel (1995).

As regards the significance to attribute to the international-isation of innovative activities for the technological develop-ment of the countries concerned, Patel and Pavitt (1991) find a positive correlation between the patents registered by large national firms and their foreign subsidiaries, on the one hand, and the technological performance of each country on the other. By contrast, the same authors show that there are no generally significant relations between the innovative activity of large foreign firms and the technological performance of the countries receiving direct foreign investments.

## 4.4. AMERICAN MULTINATIONAL FIRMS

The data set out in the previous section are unsatisfactory in many respects, and they are certainly not enough to construct

a meaningful picture of the processes of passive internationalisation undergone by the European countries. For this purpose,
in this and the next section, analysis will be restricted to
American and Japanese firms alone, since for these more
abundant information is available.

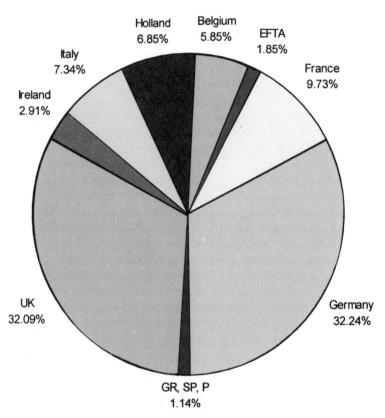

**Figure 4.2**  The Geographical Distribution of Spending on R&D by the
European Subsidiaries of American Multinational Firms, All Industries, 1989
*Notes*: The figures refer to spending on R&D by the majority-owned non-
bank affiliates of non-bank US parents. The figure for EFTA refers to
Austria, Finland, Norway, Sweden and Switzerland. The abbreviations GR,
SP and P denote Greece, Spain and Portugal respectively.
*Source*: My calculations on data from *US Department of Commerce, US
Direct Investment Abroad, 1989 Benchmark Survey, Final Result* (Table
III.I.1, column 4).

A first feature to emerge from the data on the European subsidiaries of American MNEs are the disparities in the distribution of R&D activities among the countries of Western Europe (Figure 4.2). Great Britain and Germany alone attracted around two-thirds of spending on R&D by American firms in Europe, while peripheral countries like Greece, Portugal and Spain together accounted for barely 1% of total spending. Figure 4.2 also shows the strong attraction exerted by EEC locations compared with the EFTA countries, at least as far as R&D is concerned.[2] Highly developed countries still not members of the Community, like the Scandinavian countries, Austria and Switzerland, attracted less than 2% of R&D activity by the subsidiaries of American firms in Western Europe. By contrast, small EEC countries like Belgium, Holland and Ireland, traditionally highly receptive to investment by foreign firms, accounted for a share of R&D by American firms much larger than their relative weight in EEC industry.

A very similar pattern emerges when one inspects the intensity of R&D activity by the European subsidiaries of American firms, with especial reference to the ratios between spending on R&D and number of employees shown in Figure 4.3. It is immediately evident, in fact, that innovative activity was strongly concentrated in the more developed countries of the European Union (at that time the European Economic Community). Even with equal industrial and technological development, the EEC countries apparently offered much greater locational advantages for the internationalisation of R&D activity than did the non-EEC countries. Among the countries belonging to the EEC, one notes the extremely low level of spending on R&D in the less-developed peripheral countries which had recently joined the Community: Greece, Portugal and Spain. Ireland was the EEC country in which spending on R&D was highest, probably because of the concentration of American multinational firms in the Irish electronics and computer sectors, and in its pharmaceutical industry. Although Italy attracted a relatively modest share of total spending on R&D (Figure 4.2), it apparently received American investments characterised by high technological intensity. It consequently precedes both Great Britain and France in the

---

[2] Henceforth a country's membership of the EEC or EFTA refers to 1989.

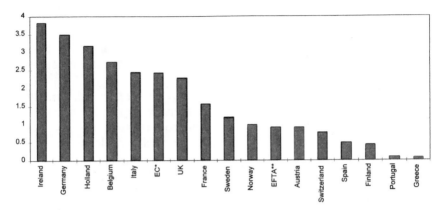

**Figure 4.3**   Spending on R&D per Employee by the European Subsidiaries of American Multinational Firms, All Industries, 1989 (in Thousands of Dollars)

*Notes*: *The figure for the European Community refers to the 10 EEC countries in the figure. **The figure for EFTA refers to the 5 nations belonging to the free trade area shown in the figure.

*Source*: My calculations on data from *US Department of Commerce, US Direct Investment Abroad, 1989 Benchmark Survey, Final Result* (Table III.I.1, column 4 and Table III.G.1, column 1).

classification table. However, as will be shown below,[3] this was the result of the greater concentration of American firms in manufacturing sectors — which accounted for the overwhelming majority of spending on R&D in every country — compared with France and Great Britain.[4]

The distribution of spending on R&D and of the indices of technological intensity reflect two principal features: the degree of technological complexity of the R&D activities transferred to each country, and the sectoral distribution of direct foreign investments. A high degree of technological intensity, in fact, may emerge both because the country hosts production phases which require greater technological inputs, and because production by local subsidiaries of foreign firms is concentrated in

---

[3] See the last row of Table 4.7.

[4] In 1989 the share of employees in manufacturing sectors in the total workforce of American firms was around 73% in Italy, compared with 62% in Great Britain and 57% in France.

sectors of higher technological intensity. To settle the question and to evidence the technological content of productive activities in each country, the various indices shown in Tables 4.2–4.7 have constructed for the six European countries for which data broken down by industry are available.

The first index, RRDCA (acronym for Revealed Research and Development Comparative Advantages), indicates the comparative advantage of a certain industry in a certain country in the location of R&D[5] activities by the subsidiaries of American multinational firms . The index was calculated using the following formula:

$$RRDCA = \frac{RD_{ij}/\sum_j RD_{ij}}{\sum_i RD_{ij}/\sum_i\sum_j RD_{ij}},$$

where RD denotes spending on R&D, and the subscripts $i$ and $j$ indicate respectively industry $i$ of country $j$. Values of the index higher (lower) than 1 indicate that the country displays, in correspondence to industry $i$, a comparative (i.e. relative to the country's other industries) advantage (disadvantage) with respect to R&D investments by American firms.

Using the same procedure, but considering the number of employees instead of spending on R&D, the RLCA index (Revealed Localisation Comparative Advantage) was constructed. Values higher (lower) than 1 indicate a comparative advantage (disadvantage) with respect to the location of productive activity by American firms.[6]

---

[5] The definition of R&D spending used in Tables 4.2–4.4 differs slightly from that used to construct the figures in this section, for two main reasons. Whereas for the figures employ the spending on R&D *by* foreign affiliates which is only available at the aggregate level, when constructing the tables spending *for* the affiliates was used. Moreover, whereas the figures refer to all branches of economic activity, the tables that follow refer only to manufacturing. These modifications — made necessary by the paucity of the data — are only minor as regards the distribution of R&D among countries. First, because most of the spending on R&D for subsidiaries is met by the subsidiaries themselves (*circa* 87% at the European level) and, second, because the bulk of spending on R&D is undertaken by subsidiaries in manufacturing sectors (circa 81%, again at the European level). However, important national differences exist, such as those described above as regards France, Great Britain and Italy.

[6] The figure for employees also includes those engaged in R&D. However, since these employees are generally very few in number compared with the total workforce, this should not affect the comparison between the RRDCA and RLCA indices.

Table 4.2   Comparative Advantages of the European Countries in the Location of R&D Activities by American Multinational Firms, manufacturing Industries, 1989

| | RRDCA | | | | | |
|---|---|---|---|---|---|---|
| | France | Germany | Italy | Holland | Switzerland | UK |
| Food and kindred products | 1.58 | 0.67 | 0.71 | 1.38 | 0.00 | 1.49 |
| Chemicals and allied products | 1.56 | 0.50 | 1.50 | 0.67 | 1.01 | 1.28 |
| Industrial chemicals and synthetics | 1.50 | 0.73 | n.a. | 2.55 | 0.00 | 0.63 |
| Drugs | 1.47 | 0.42 | 1.69 | 0.25 | 1.27 | 1.49 |
| Soap, cleaners and toilette goods | n.a. | n.a. | 0.87 | 0.11 | 0.86 | 1.41 |
| Agricultural chemicals | 0.00 | 0.00 | 4.20 | 5.67 | 0.00 | 0.88 |
| Chemical products n.e.c. | n.a. | n.a. | n.a. | 0.81 | 1.26 | 0.76 |
| Primary and fabricated metals | 0.79 | 1.01 | 0.00 | 1.96 | 6.49 | 0.98 |
| Primary metal goods | 0.00 | 1.15 | 0.00 | 0.00 | 0.00 | 1.41 |
| Fabricated metal products | 0.87 | 1.00 | 0.00 | 2.16 | 4.77 | 0.93 |
| Machinery, except electrical | 1.56 | 0.73 | 1.67 | 0.23 | 1.56 | 0.62 |
| Farm and garden machinery | 0.00 | n.a. | 0.00 | 0.00 | 0.00 | 0.13 |
| Construction, mining and materials handling machinery | n.a. | 0.36 | 0.00 | 0.94 | 0.00 | 0.77 |
| Office and computing machines | n.a. | n.a. | n.a. | 0.05 | 0.00 | 0.61 |
| Machinery n.e.c. | 1.77 | 0.66 | n.a. | 0.54 | 5.88 | 0.86 |

| | | | | | |
|---|---|---|---|---|---|
| Electric and electronic equipment | 0.35 | 0.69 | 0.71 | n.a. | 0.82 | n.a. |
| Household appliances | 0.75 | n.a. | 0.59 | 0.53 | 0.00 | 0.68 |
| Electronic components and accessories | 0.71 | 1.22 | 1.78 | 0.90 | 0.77 | 0.68 |
| Transport equipment | 0.32 | 1.79 | 0.46 | 0.03 | 0.00 | n.a. |
| Other manufacturing industries | 1.34 | 0.68 | 1.04 | n.a. | 2.76 | n.a. |
| Tobacco products | 0.00 | 0.00 | 2.40 | 0.00 | 33.36 | 3.52 |
| Textile products and apparel | 0.53 | n.a. | 0.00 | 1.51 | 0.00 | 0.70 |
| Lumber, wood, furniture and fixtures | 0.00 | 1.44 | 4.20 | 0.00 | 0.00 | 0.00 |
| Paper and allied products | 0.00 | 1.36 | 0.00 | 0.00 | 0.00 | 0.93 |
| Printing and publishing | 0.00 | 0.00 | 0.00 | 0.00 | 0.00 | 3.52 |
| Rubber products | 2.37 | 0.24 | 3.27 | 0.42 | 3.24 | 0.29 |
| Glass products | 2.67 | 0.00 | 0.00 | 0.00 | 0.00 | 1.32 |
| Stone, clay and other nonmetallic mineral products | 1.33 | n.a. | 0.00 | 0.00 | 0.00 | 0.44 |
| Instruments and related products | 2.09 | 0.98 | 1.55 | 0.64 | 2.25 | 0.97 |

*Notes*: n.a. = not available. The indexes have been constructed with reference to total spending on R&D by subsidiaries operating in manufacturing industry. Since the original data do not specify the exact amount of spending when it was less than $500,000, this value has been set equal to 0.

*Source*: My calculations on data from *US Department of Commerce, US Direct Investment Abroad, 1989 Benchmark Survey, Final Result* (Table III.I.4).

Table 4.3   Comparative Advantages of European Countries in the Location of Production Activities by American Multinational Firms, manufacturing Industries, 1989

| | RLCA | | | | | |
|---|---|---|---|---|---|---|
| | France | Germany | Italy | Holland | Switzerland | UK |
| Food and kindred products | 0.85 | 0.49 | 1.00 | 1.74 | 1.63 | 1.06 |
| Chemicals and allied products | 1.13 | 0.75 | 1.38 | 1.61 | 0.74 | 0.84 |
| Industrial chemicals and synthetics | 0.94 | 0.91 | 0.63 | 3.70 | 0.20 | 0.65 |
| Drugs | 1.35 | 0.59 | 1.99 | 0.30 | 1.18 | 0.88 |
| Soap, cleaners and toilette goods | 1.00 | 0.98 | 1.22 | 0.93 | 0.95 | 0.92 |
| Agricultural chemicals | 1.99 | 0.16 | 3.77 | 2.68 | 0.00 | 0.41 |
| Chemical products n.e.c. | 1.18 | 0.44 | 1.58 | 1.62 | 0.43 | 1.07 |
| Primary and fabricated metals | 0.87 | 1.24 | 0.48 | 1.97 | 0.81 | 1.06 |
| Primary metal goods | 0.99 | 0.56 | n.a. | 1.96 | 0.00 | 1.06 |
| Fabricated metal products | 0.85 | 1.36 | n.a. | 1.98 | 0.95 | 1.06 |
| Machinery, except electrical | 1.25 | 0.97 | 1.33 | 0.73 | 1.26 | 1.04 |
| Farm and garden machinery | 0.04 | n.a. | 0.06 | 0.00 | 0.00 | n.a. |
| Construction, mining and materials handling machinery | n.a. | 0.52 | 0.34 | 0.78 | 1.30 | 0.98 |
| Office and computing machines | n.a. | n.a. | n.a. | n.a. | n.a. | 0.84 |
| Machinery n.e.c. | 1.13 | 0.76 | n.a. | n.a. | n.a. | n.a. |

| | | | | | | |
|---|---|---|---|---|---|---|
| Electric and electronic equipment | 0.73 | 0.82 | 0.79 | 1.45 | 1.84 | 1.13 |
| Household appliances | n.a. | n.a. | 0.41 | n.a. | 0.93 | 1.10 |
| Electronic components and accessories | 0.97 | 1.05 | 1.14 | 0.54 | 1.75 | 0.95 |
| Transport equipment | 0.39 | 1.74 | 0.77 | 0.11 | 0.00 | 0.94 |
| Other manufacturing industries | 1.45 | 0.73 | 0.88 | 0.93 | 1.37 | 1.04 |
| Tobacco products | 0.09 | n.a. | 0.51 | 3.41 | n.a. | n.a. |
| Textile products and apparel | 2.03 | 0.41 | 0.24 | 0.47 | 0.00 | 1.08 |
| Lumber, wood, furniture and fixtures | 0.33 | 1.13 | 1.41 | 0.29 | 1.80 | 1.12 |
| Paper and allied products | 1.69 | 0.89 | 0.62 | 0.72 | 0.00 | 1.04 |
| Printing and publishing | 0.79 | 0.26 | 0.68 | 1.42 | 0.87 | 1.92 |
| Rubber products | 1.70 | 0.69 | 0.81 | 0.94 | 1.27 | 0.68 |
| Glass products | 2.51 | 0.08 | n.a. | 0.14 | 0.88 | 1.05 |
| Stone, clay and other nonmetallic mineral products | 1.74 | 0.95 | n.a. | 0.60 | 0.00 | 0.61 |
| Instruments and related products | 1.50 | 0.80 | 1.12 | 1.26 | 1.72 | 1.11 |

*Notes*: n.a. = not available. The indexes have been constructed with reference to the total number of employees of subsidiaries operating in manufacturing industry. Since the original data did not specify the exact amount of employees when they were fewer than 50 units, this value has been set equal to 0.
*Source*: My calculations on data from *US Department of Commerce, US Direct Investment Abroad, 1989 Benchmark Survey, Final Result* (Table III.G.4).

Table 4.4   Comparative Advantages of European Countries in Terms of the Technological Intensity of the Subsidiaries of American Multinational Firms, manufacturing Industries, 1989

| | RRDCA/RLCA | | | | | |
| --- | --- | --- | --- | --- | --- | --- |
| | France | Germany | Italy | Holland | Switzerland | UK |
| Food and kindred products | 1.85 | 1.36 | 0.71 | 0.80 | 0.00 | 1.41 |
| Chemicals and allied products | 1.37 | 0.67 | 1.09 | 0.42 | 1.37 | 1.52 |
| Industrial chemicals and synthetics | 1.60 | 0.80 | n.a. | 0.69 | 0.00 | 0.97 |
| Drugs | 1.09 | 0.71 | 0.85 | 0.81 | 1.07 | 1.70 |
| Soap, cleaners and toilette goods | n.a. | n.a. | 0.72 | 0.12 | 0.91 | 1.53 |
| Agricultural chemicals | 0.00 | 0.00 | 1.12 | 2.12 | * | 2.15 |
| Chemical products n.e.c. | n.a. | n.a. | n.a. | 0.50 | 2.90 | 0.71 |
| Primary and fabricated metals | 0.91 | 0.82 | 0.00 | 0.99 | 8.04 | 0.92 |
| Primary metal goods | 0.00 | 2.07 | n.a. | 0.00 | * | 1.33 |
| Fabricated metal products | 1.03 | 0.73 | n.a. | 1.09 | 5.03 | 0.88 |
| Machinery, except electrical | 1.26 | 0.76 | 1.25 | 0.31 | 1.24 | 0.59 |
| Farm and garden machinery | 0.00 | n.a. | 0.00 | * | * | n.a. |
| Construction, mining and materials handling machinery | n.a. | 0.69 | 0.00 | 1.22 | 0.00 | 0.78 |
| Office and computing machines | n.a. | n.a. | n.a. | n.a. | n.a. | 0.73 |
| Machinery n.e.c. | 1.56 | 0.88 | n.a. | n.a. | n.a. | n.a. |

| | | | | | |
|---|---|---|---|---|---|
| Electric and electronic equipment | 0.48 | 0.83 | 0.90 | n.a. | 0.45 | n.a. |
| Household appliances | n.a. | n.a. | 1.44 | n.a. | 0.00 | 0.62 |
| Electronic components and accessories | 0.73 | 1.16 | 1.56 | 1.68 | 0.44 | 0.71 |
| Transport equipment | 0.82 | 1.03 | 0.60 | 0.30 | * | n.a. |
| Other manufacturing industries | 0.93 | 0.94 | 1.18 | n.a. | 2.02 | n.a. |
| Tobacco products | 0.00 | n.a. | 4.68 | 0.00 | n.a. | n.a. |
| Textile products and apparel | 0.26 | n.a. | 0.00 | 3.20 | * | 0.65 |
| Lumber, wood, furniture and fixtures | 0.00 | 1.27 | 2.97 | 0.00 | 0.00 | 0.00 |
| Paper and allied products | 0.00 | 1.54 | 0.00 | 0.00 | * | 0.89 |
| Printing and publishing | 0.00 | 0.00 | 0.00 | 0.00 | 0.00 | 1.83 |
| Rubber products | 1.40 | 0.35 | 4.01 | 0.45 | 2.55 | 0.43 |
| Glass products | 1.06 | 0.00 | n.a. | 0.00 | 0.00 | 1.25 |
| Stone, clay and other nonmetallic mineral products | 0.77 | n.a. | n.a. | 0.00 | * | 0.73 |
| Instruments and related products | 1.40 | 1.21 | 1.38 | 0.51 | 1.31 | 0.88 |

*Notes:* n.a. = not available. The symbol * indicates that there are no affiliates of American firms operating in the industry of the country considered.

*Source:* My calculations on data from *US Department of Commerce, US Direct Investment Abroad, 1989 Benchmark Survey, Final Result* (Tables III.I.4 and III.G.4).

Table 4.5   Geographical Distribution of R&D Spending by the Subsidiaries of American Multinational Firms, manufacturing Industries, 1989

| | % R&D per nation out of industry total | | | | | |
|---|---|---|---|---|---|---|
| | France | Germany | Italy | Holland | Switzerland | UK |
| Food and kindred products | 14.79 | 23.24 | 4.23 | 9.15 | 0.00 | 42.25 |
| Chemicals and allied products | 14.58 | 17.45 | 8.94 | 4.43 | 0.87 | 36.37 |
| Industrial chemicals and synthetics | 14.04 | 25.28 | n.a. | 16.85 | 0.00 | 17.98 |
| Drugs | 13.82 | 14.50 | 10.03 | 1.63 | 1.08 | 42.28 |
| Soap, cleaners and toilette goods | n.a. | n.a. | 5.19 | 0.74 | 0.74 | 40.00 |
| Agricultural chemicals | 0.00 | 0.00 | 25.00 | 37.50 | 0.00 | 25.00 |
| Chemical products n.e.c. | n.a. | n.a. | n.a. | 5.38 | 1.08 | 21.51 |
| Primary and fabricated metals | 7.41 | 35.19 | 0.00 | 12.96 | 5.56 | 27.78 |
| Primary metal goods | 0.00 | 40.00 | 0.00 | 0.00 | 0.00 | 40.00 |
| Fabricated metal products | 8.16 | 34.69 | 0.00 | 14.29 | 4.08 | 26.53 |
| Machinery, except electrical | 14.67 | 25.33 | 9.90 | 1.52 | 1.33 | 17.52 |
| Farm and garden machinery | 0.00 | n.a. | 0.00 | 0.00 | 0.00 | 3.75 |
| Construction, mining and materials handling machinery | n.a. | 12.50 | 0.00 | 6.25 | 0.00 | 21.88 |
| Office and computing machines | n.a. | n.a. | n.a. | 0.36 | 0.00 | 17.45 |
| Machinery n.e.c. | 16.55 | 23.02 | n.a. | 3.60 | 5.04 | 24.46 |

| | | | | | | |
|---|---|---|---|---|---|---|
| Electric and electronic equipment | 3.27 | 23.83 | 4.21 | n.a. | 0.70 | n.a. |
| Household appliances | 7.02 | n.a. | 3.51 | 3.51 | 0.00 | 19.30 |
| Electronic components and accessories | 6.62 | 42.38 | 10.60 | 5.96 | 0.66 | 19.21 |
| Transport equipment | 3.03 | 62.26 | 2.73 | 0.22 | 0.00 | n.a. |
| Other manufacturing industries | 12.57 | 23.68 | 6.19 | n.a. | 2.37 | n.a. |
| Tobacco products | 0.00 | 5.56 | 0.00 | 11.11 | 38.89 | 38.89 |
| Textile products and apparel | 5.00 | n.a. | 0.00 | 10.00 | 0.00 | 20.00 |
| Lumber, wood, furniture and fixtures | 0.00 | 50.00 | 25.00 | 0.00 | 0.00 | 0.00 |
| Paper and allied products | 0.00 | 47.37 | 0.00 | 0.00 | 0.00 | 26.32 |
| Printing and publishing | 0.00 | 0.00 | 0.00 | 0.00 | 0.00 | 100.00 |
| Rubber products | 22.22 | 8.33 | 19.44 | 2.78 | 2.78 | 8.33 |
| Glass products | 25.00 | 0.00 | 0.00 | 0.00 | 0.00 | 37.50 |
| Stone, clay and other nonmetallic mineral products | 12.50 | n.a. | 0.00 | 0.00 | 0.00 | 12.50 |
| Instruments and related products | 19.62 | 33.85 | 9.23 | 4.23 | 1.92 | 27.69 |
| All manufacturing industries | 9.37 | 34.71 | 5.95 | 6.61 | 0.86 | 28.43 |

*Notes:* n.a. = not available. Since the original data did not specify the exact amount of spending when it was less than $500,000, this value has been set equal to 0.

*Source:* My calculations on data from *US Department of Commerce, US Direct Investment Abroad, 1989 Benchmark Survey, Final Result* (Table III.I.4).

Table 4.6  Geographical Distribution of Employees of the Subsidiaries of American Multinational Firms, manufacturing Industries, 1989

| | % employee per nation out of industry total | | | | | |
| --- | --- | --- | --- | --- | --- | --- |
| | France | Germany | Italy | Holland | Switzerland | UK |
| Food and kindred products | 10.71 | 12.53 | 7.72 | 8.13 | 1.24 | 32.37 |
| Chemicals and allied products | 14.24 | 19.05 | 10.69 | 7.53 | 0.56 | 25.80 |
| Industrial chemicals and synthetics | 11.79 | 23.12 | 4.90 | 17.30 | 0.15 | 19.91 |
| Drugs | 16.94 | 15.02 | 15.40 | 1.41 | 0.90 | 26.83 |
| Soap, cleaners and toilette goods | 12.52 | 24.86 | 9.44 | 4.36 | 0.73 | 28.13 |
| Agricultural chemicals | 25.00 | 4.17 | 29.17 | 12.50 | 0.00 | 12.50 |
| Chemical products n.e.c. | 14.85 | 11.22 | 12.21 | 7.59 | 0.33 | 32.67 |
| Primary and fabricated metals | 10.95 | 31.61 | 3.69 | 9.23 | 0.62 | 32.35 |
| Primary metal goods | 12.50 | 14.17 | n.a. | 9.17 | 0.00 | 32.50 |
| Fabricated metal products | 10.68 | 34.63 | n.a. | 9.24 | 0.72 | 32.32 |
| Machinery, except electrical | 15.66 | 24.54 | 10.28 | 3.43 | 0.96 | 31.84 |
| Farm and garden machinery | 0.46 | n.a. | 0.46 | 0.00 | 0.00 | n.a. |
| Construction, mining and materials handling machinery | n.a. | 13.20 | 2.64 | 3.63 | 0.99 | 30.03 |
| Office and computing machines | n.a. | n.a. | n.a. | n.a. | n.a. | 25.86 |
| Machinery n.e.c. | 14.27 | 19.23 | n.a. | n.a. | n.a. | n.a. |

| | | | | | |
|---|---|---|---|---|---|
| Electric and electronic equipment | 9.24 | 20.92 | 6.09 | 6.79 | 1.40 | 34.50 |
| Household appliances | n.a. | n.a. | 3.18 | n.a. | 0.71 | 33.57 |
| Electronic components and accessories | 12.19 | 26.71 | 8.85 | 2.50 | 1.34 | 29.22 |
| Transport equipment | 4.97 | 44.25 | 5.95 | 0.52 | 0.00 | 28.79 |
| Other manufacturing industries | 18.18 | 18.50 | 6.85 | 4.35 | 1.04 | 31.91 |
| Tobacco products | 1.14 | n.a. | 3.98 | 15.91 | n.a. | n.a. |
| Textile products and apparel | 25.55 | 10.41 | 1.89 | 2.21 | 0.00 | 33.12 |
| Lumber, wood, furniture and fixtures | 4.11 | 28.77 | 10.96 | 1.37 | 1.37 | 34.25 |
| Paper and allied products | 21.29 | 22.55 | 4.80 | 3.34 | 0.00 | 31.73 |
| Printing and publishing | 9.93 | 6.62 | 5.30 | 6.62 | 0.66 | 58.94 |
| Rubber products | 21.36 | 17.48 | 6.31 | 4.37 | 0.97 | 20.87 |
| Glass products | 31.54 | 2.01 | n.a. | 0.67 | 0.67 | 32.21 |
| Stone, clay and other nonmetallic mineral products | 21.91 | 24.16 | n.a. | 2.81 | 0.00 | 18.54 |
| Instruments and related products | 18.82 | 20.41 | 8.71 | 5.90 | 1.31 | 34.08 |
| All manufacturing industries | 12.58 | 25.42 | 7.75 | 4.67 | 0.76 | 30.63 |

*Notes:* n.a. = not available. Since the original data did not specify the exact number of employees when fewer than 50 units, this value has been set equal to 0.

*Source:* My calculations on data from *US Department of Commerce, US Direct Investment Abroad, 1989 Benchmark Survey, Final Result* (Table III.G.4).

Table 4.7   Absolute Advantages of European Countries in Terms of the Technological Intensity of the Subsidiaries of American Multinational Firms, manufacturing Industries, 1989

| | RRIAA | | | | | |
| --- | --- | --- | --- | --- | --- | --- |
| | France | Germany | Italy | Holland | Switzerland | UK |
| Food and kindred products | 1.38 | 1.85 | 0.55 | 1.13 | 0.00 | 1.31 |
| Chemicals and allied products | 1.02 | 0.92 | 0.84 | 0.59 | 1.54 | 1.41 |
| Industrial chemicals and synthetics | 1.19 | 1.09 | n.a. | 0.97 | 0.00 | 0.90 |
| Drugs | 0.82 | 0.97 | 0.65 | 1.15 | 1.21 | 1.58 |
| Soap, cleaners and toilette goods | n.a. | n.a. | 0.55 | 0.17 | 1.02 | 1.42 |
| Agricultural chemicals | 0.00 | 0.00 | 0.86 | 3.00 | * | 2.00 |
| Chemical products n.e.c. | n.a. | n.a. | n.a. | 0.71 | 3.26 | 0.66 |
| Primary and fabricated metals | 0.68 | 1.11 | 0.00 | 1.41 | 9.03 | 0.86 |
| Primary metal goods | 0.00 | 2.82 | n.a. | 0.00 | * | 1.23 |
| Fabricated metal products | 0.76 | 1.00 | n.a. | 1.55 | 5.66 | 0.82 |
| Machinery, except electrical | 0.94 | 1.03 | 0.96 | 0.44 | 1.39 | 0.55 |
| Farm and garden machinery | 0.00 | n.a. | 0.00 | * | * | n.a. |
| Construction, mining and materials handling machinery | n.a. | 0.95 | 0.00 | 1.72 | 0.00 | 0.73 |
| Office and computing machines | n.a. | n.a. | n.a. | n.a. | n.a. | 0.67 |
| Machinery n.e.c. | 1.16 | 1.20 | n.a. | n.a. | n.a. | n.a. |

| | | | | | | |
|---|---|---|---|---|---|---|
| Electric and electronic equipment | 0.35 | 1.14 | 0.69 | n.a. | 0.50 | n.a. |
| Household appliances | n.a. | n.a. | 1.10 | n.a. | 0.00 | 0.57 |
| Electronic components and accessories | 0.54 | 1.59 | 1.20 | 2.38 | 0.50 | 0.66 |
| Transport equipment | 0.61 | 1.41 | 0.46 | 0.42 | * | n.a. |
| Other manufacturing industries | 0.69 | 1.28 | 0.90 | n.a. | 2.27 | n.a. |
| Tobacco products | 0.00 | n.a. | 3.59 | 0.00 | n.a. | n.a. |
| Textile products and apparel | 0.20 | n.a. | 0.00 | 4.53 | * | 0.60 |
| Lumber, wood, furniture and fixtures | 0.00 | 1.74 | 2.28 | 0.00 | 0.00 | 0.00 |
| Paper and allied products | 0.00 | 2.10 | 0.00 | 0.00 | * | 0.83 |
| Printing and publishing | 0.00 | 0.00 | 0.00 | 0.00 | 0.00 | 1.70 |
| Rubber products | 1.04 | 0.48 | 3.08 | 0.64 | 2.86 | 0.40 |
| Glass products | 0.79 | 0.00 | n.a. | 0.00 | 0.00 | 1.16 |
| Stone, clay and other nonmetallic mineral products | 0.57 | n.a. | n.a. | 0.00 | * | 0.67 |
| Instruments and related products | 1.04 | 1.66 | 1.06 | 0.72 | 1.47 | 0.81 |
| All manufacturing industries | 0.75 | 1.37 | 0.77 | 1.42 | 1.12 | 0.93 |

*Notes:* n.a. = not available. The symbol * indicates that there are no affiliates of American firms operating in the industry of the country considered.

*Source:* My calculations on data from *US Department of Commerce, US Direct Investment Abroad, 1989 Benchmark Survey, Final Result* (Tables III.I.4 and III.G.4).

Table 4.4 sets out the RRDCA/RLCA ratios. Values higher (lower) than 1 indicate that technological intensity (i.e. spending on R&D per employee) in American firms in industry $i$ of country $j$ is greater (smaller) than the average technological intensity of American firms operating in that country.[7]

As well as these indices, which refer to the comparative advantages of the industrial sectors of a country, three further indices of absolute advantage were constructed. The first two of them measure the degree of attractiveness (i.e. the locational advantages) of a certain national industry compared with the other European countries as regards the R&D and productive activities of American firms in Europe. These indices were constructed simply by calculating each country's share of the European total of spending on R&D (Table 4.5) and of employees (Table 4.6) of American firms in Europe in each industrial sector. The third index of absolute advantage, RRIAA (Revealed Research Intensity Absolute Advantage), denotes a country's absolute advantage in terms of R&D spending/employees in American subsidiaries compared with the European average (Table 4.7). This index was constructed by calculating the ratio between the two indices just described. Values higher (lower) than 1 indicate that the intensity of R&D activity by American subsidiaries in national industry is greater (lesser) than the average intensity of American firms in Europe in the same industrial sector.

The reason for setting out all these indices — which may at first sight be confusing, given the abundance of figures provided — is that both comparative and absolute advantages are important for assessment of the effect of international production on the destination countries and, more generally, of the changes that it induces in the industrial and technological structure of the European countries through the international reallocation of productive and innovative activities. Comparative advantages, in fact, express the relative attractiveness of each national industrial sector purged of the 'nation' effect, i.e. the role performed by the country *per se* as the base for international production and R&D activities by American

---

[7] It can be shown in simple mathematical steps, in fact, that the RRDCA/RLCA ratio is equal to the index yielded by the above formula if spending on R&D is replaced by spending on R&D per employee.

multinationals. By contrast, the absolute advantages denote the direction and extent of the reallocation of productive and innovative activities among the various European countries.

The considerable amount of information provided by Tables 4.2–4.7 can give cause for much thought. In what follows, however, I shall concentrate on aspects most relevant to the theme of this book.

A first finding is that a country's comparative advantages of in terms of the location of productive activities (Table 4.3) do not generally correspond to its comparative advantages in terms of the location of R&D activities by American multinational firms (Table 4.2). Nor is this disproportion simply due to the fact that different activities require different quantities of technological inputs, since the classification of productive sectors in terms of technological intensity differs considerably from country to country (Table 4.4). This gives rise to a heterogeneous distribution of the absolute advantages of a country in terms of the R&D/employee index (Table 4.7), indicating that the technological intensity of American subsidiaries varies substantially from one country to another and internally to the same production sector, thereby creating or reinforcing uneven patterns of technological and industrial development. This is evident with respect to both the competitiveness of national industrial systems, since these are *directly* and *indirectly*[8] influenced by the technological content of production by foreign multinational firms, and to the reinforcement of specific paths of sectoral specialisation — as results from the comparative advantages of countries in terms of the location of production activities (i.e. from the distribution of employees).

Secondly, as regards the location of both production activities and R&D, the structure of comparative advantages does not always correspond to the known strengths and weakness of a country's industrial and innovative system; indeed, in many cases, the multi-nationalisation strategies pursued by American firms do not match the characteristics of the productive and innovative structure of the host country. An example of correspondence between the competitive advantages of a destination country's industry and the multinationalisation strategies of American firms is provided by the pharmaceutical industry.

---

[8] Cf. Section 4.3.

The competitive advantage in terms of technological development acquired by British industry during the 1980s is well
reflected in the comparative advantages of the British pharmaceutical industry in the location of R&D activities by American
multinationals (Table 4.2) and in its comparative advantages in
terms of technological intensity (Table 4.4). It is also reflected in
Britain's absolute advantages compared with its main European
competitors in terms of share of overall R&D activity by
American firms in Europe (more than 40%, Table 4.5) and in its
role as European leader as regards the technological intensity
of American firms in the sector (Table 4.7).[9] An example, of a
mismatch between the competitive advantages of a national
industrial system and the strategies of the American multinationals is instead provided by the textiles and clothing industry.
In this case, despite the well-known competitive advantages of
the Italian industry, both the structure of its comparative
advantages (Tables 4.2–4.4) and absolute advantages (Tables
4.5–4.7) highlight Italy's very marginal role both as a productive base, where it is outstripped by France, Germany and
Great Britain, and as a base for innovative activity by American MNEs, which are entirely absent from the country.

The last rows of Tables 4.5–4.7 give a good idea of the overall
impact, in terms of technological content and employment, of
manufacturing activity by American firms in the six countries
considered. Germany and Great Britain are by far the main
productive and innovative centres in Europe for American firms.
However, although Great Britain ranks higher than Germany in
terms of employees, the opposite is the case of spending on
R&D, which confirms Germany's position as the European
leader in the field of innovation and high-tech production.
France and Italy occupy a very marginal role in the multi-
nationalisation strategies of American firms, especially if one
takes account of the size of these two countries and of the fact
that they host, on average, activities with relatively low technological intensity (Table 4.7) compared with the other countries
considered. By contrast, very good performances are achieved by
Holland and Switzerland, countries which either host productive
and innovative activities in proportions much greater than their
size (Holland) or are specialised in high-tech activities (both
countries). In some cases, the disparities in the distribution of
productiveand innovative activities by American firms in the

---

[9] Another good example is the German automobile industry.

European countries are reflected in the structure of the comparative advantages of each country. To cite the example of Italy
again, this country displays a comparative advantage as regards
the location of high-tech activities in its electrical appliances
sector (Table 4.4), since this is a sector in which Italy is renowned
for the competitiveness of its productive system at the European
level. Yet, in absolute terms, Italy's share is very modest, since
it attracts only 4% of spending on R&D and 3% of employees
(Tables 4.5 and 4.6), even though it enjoys an absolute advantage in terms of technological intensity (Table 4.7).

The role of the American MNEs in the productive and
technological development of the European countries is determined both by the amount and quality of activities by these
firms, and by their influence on national productive and innovative structures. Accordingly, Figure 4.4 shows the share of total
R&D spending by the subsidiaries of American firms in the
business sectors of 16 European countries. Although the figures
should be interpreted with a certain amount of caution — given

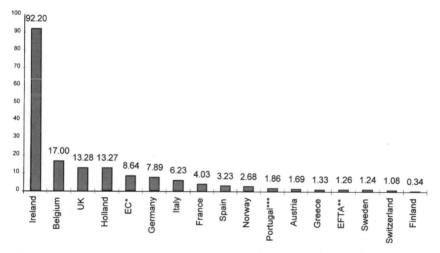

**Figure 4.4** Percentage share of spending on National R&D (BERD) by the
European Subsidiaries of American Multinational Firms, All Industries, 1989
*Notes*: *The figure for the European Community refers to the 10 EEC
countries shown. **The figure for EFTA refers to the five countries belonging
to the free trade area listed. ***Since the figure for Portuguese BERD in 1989
is unavailable, the average of the two adjacent years has been used.
*Source*: My calculations on data from *US Department of Commerce, US Direct Investment Abroad, 1989 Benchmark Survey, Final Result* (Table III.I.1).

possible discrepancies in data-gathering and processing methods — they highlight that the importance of participation by American firms in national innovative systems varies considerably among countries. At one extreme stands Ireland, a country in which more than 90% if R&D activity is controlled by American firms; at the other, the Nordic countries, where the percentage ranges from Norway's 2.68% to Finland's 0.34%. Even ignoring the extreme case of Ireland, R&D activity by American subsidiaries reaches significant proportions in most of the EEC countries, with an average percentage higher than 8% (Ireland included) and levels higher than 10% in Belgium, Great Britain and Holland. Bearing in mind that the figures concern only the majority-owned subsidiaries of American multinationals, it is evident that the control exercised by American firms over the innovative activities of EEC countries is actually greater than appears from Figure 4.4.

Although the amount of spending on R&D per employee is a good indicator of the technological activity of American

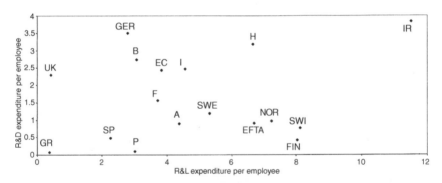

**Figure 4.5** Spending on R&D per Employee and Spending on Royalties and Licence Fees per Employee by the European Subsidiaries of American Multinational Firms, All Industries, 1989 (Thousands of Dollars)

*Notes*: A = Austria, B = Belgium, F = France, FIN = Finland, UK = United Kingdom, GER = Germany, GR = Greece, I = Italy, IR = Ireland, H = Holland, P = Portugal, NOR = Norway, SP = Spain, SWE = Sweden, SWI = Switzerland. The figure for the European Community refers to the 10 EEC countries shown. The figure for EFTA refers to the five countries listed belonging to the free trade area listed.

*Source*: My calculations on data from *US Department of Commerce, US Direct Investment Abroad, 1989 Benchmark Survey, Final Result* (Tables III.I.1, III.I.7, III.G.1).

affiliates, it tells us very little about the actual type of activity undertaken. In particular, it does not specify whether this spending corresponds to genuine innovative activity, or whether it concerns the straightforward adaptation of the multinational firm's existing technologies to the consumer tastes and technical standards of the European market.

Information on these matters can be obtained by setting R&D spending per employee in relation to payments for royalties and licences, again per employee (Figure 4.5). Figure 4.6 gives the ratios between these two variables in order to facilitate comparison. The idea behind the two figures is that the larger the amount of spending on R&D/employees relative to payments for royalties and licences/employees, the greater the relative importance of the development of local technological lines compared with activity involving the adaptation of imported technologies to the requirements of the European market.

A first finding to emerge from Figures 4.5 and 4.6 is that in all the European countries, with the exception of Great Britain and Germany, the subsidiaries of American MNEs devote more

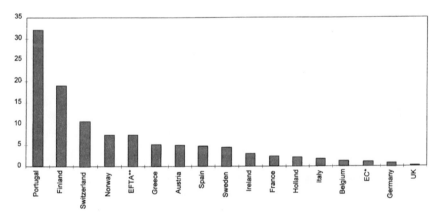

**Figure 4.6** Ratio Between Spending on Royalties and Licence Fees and on R&D by the European Subsidiaries of American Multinational Firms, All Industries, 1989

*Notes*: The figure for the European Community refers to the 10 EEC countries shown. The figure for EFTA refers to the five countries belonging to the free trade area.

*Source*: My calculations on data from *US Department of Commerce, US Direct Investment Abroad, 1989 Benchmark Survey, Final Result* (Tables III.I.1, III.I.7, III.G.1).

resources to the importing of technology than to R&D. Bearing in mind that a proportion of R&D spending probably goes on minor modifications made to already developed technology, one deduces that in the majority of the European countries the exploitation of indigenous lines of technological development by American firms is probably rather modest. However, it tends to be relatively much greater in the more developed EEC countries, compared with those lying outside the regional bloc, or with the peripheral countries like Greece, Portugal and Spain. As regards these latter, one explanation for the greater propensity of American subsidiaries to import technology rather than produce it *in loco* may be, besides the relative lag in these countries' technological development, their recent entry into the Community. EEC membership has in fact stimulated new investments by American firms, and these investments have probably required massive transfers of technology, whilst R&D by their subsidiaries is still limited due to their recent creation.

These findings are apparently confirmed by inspection of the earnings accruing to the European subsidiaries of American firms from the granting of licences on their patents (Figure 4.7).

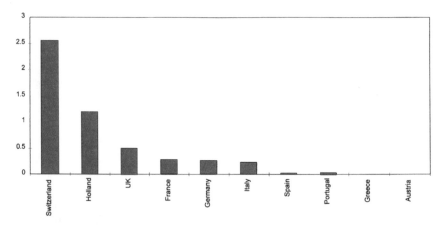

**Figure 4.7**   Earnings from Royalties and Licence Fees per Employee by the European Subsidiaries of American Multinational Firms, all industries, 1989 (Thousands of Dollars)
*Source*: My calculations on data from *US Department of Commerce, US Direct Investment Abroad, 1989 Benchmark Survey, Final Result* (Tables III.I.7, III.G.1).

The role of American subsidiaries in the production of technology seems to be positively correlated with the host country's degree of development and with its tradition as a base for international production by American firms. This confirms the existence of an *evolutionary* pattern in the behaviour of the foreign subsidiaries of MNEs, which tend over time to grow increasingly independent of the parent-company (Cantwell, 1989). This latter feature would explain the high values obtained for Switzerland, Holland and to a certain extent Great Britain; values that otherwise could not be accounted for on the basis of the level of technological development of these countries compared with others. Also significant is Austria's bottom position in the classification, below countries like Portugal and Greece, which is probably due to that country's marginal role as a European productive base for American multinationals.

## 4.5. JAPANESE INVESTMENTS IN EUROPE

The growing participation of Japanese firms in the productive systems of the European countries is perhaps one of the most salient aspects of the internationalisation of production in the past decade. On the basis of figures provided by the annual surveys conducted by the Japan External Trade Organisation (JETRO) — which probably omit a large number of small and medium-sized firms with Japanese shareholdings[10] — between December 1983 and December 1994 the number of manufacturing firms with a shareholding by Japanese investors greater than or equal to 10% rose from 186 to 718: an increase of more than 350% (JETRO, 1995).

As in the case of American firms, the Japanese presence in the European countries is heterogeneous as regards both the distribution of productive activities and the location of innovative ones (Figure 4.8). Great Britain, France and Germany alone attract almost 60% of Japanese firms, more than 65% of those with R&D centres, and around 70% of independent R&D centres. Although in the period considered (1984–1994) Italy

---

[10] This can be directly verified in the Italian case. Whereas at the end of 1993 JETRO listed 46 firms with Japanese majority shareholders in Italy, another source (this too probably not exhaustive) puts the number of the affiliates of Japanese firms at 53 (Cominotti and Mariotti, 1994).

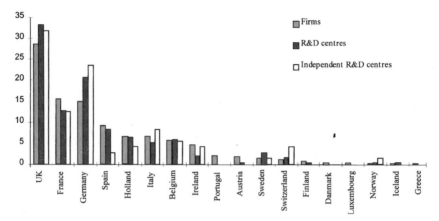

**Figure 4.8**   Geographical Distribution of Japanese Firms and R&D Centres in European Countries, 1994 (Percentage Values)
*Source*: My calculations on data from JETRO (1995).

more than tripled the number of Japanese firms on its national territory, it was preceded in this particular classification by countries with a lower level of development (Spain) or of much smaller size (Holland), although it had a larger number of independent R&D countries than both of them.

These characteristics of Japanese participation in the industries of the various European countries midway through the 1990s result from the different strategies of internationalisation implemented in past decades. According to the reconstruction proposed by one of the most widely cited authors (Dunning, 1994b), prior to 1984 Japanese FDI in Europe and in the USA was intended mainly to defend the market shares of the leading sectors of Japanese industry against the protectionist measures threatened by the governments of those countries, given their substantial trade deficits with Japan. The principal task assigned to the majority of the European subsidiaries of Japanese firms was to set up plants for the assembly of parts and components imported from Japan, or if rules of origin were in force, purchased from other Japanese firms operating in Europe. In the years that followed, a series of factors — mainly the increased value of the Yen, the revival of European industry, and the ongoing process of European integration — engendered major changes in the strategies of the Japanese multinationals. On the one hand, the attractiveness of the European countries increased in terms of outlet markets. On the other, European industry assumed a crucial role in the development of new scientific and technological knowledge. Among the principal consequences of these changes were: (i) the increasing involvement of the subsidiaries of Japanese firms in domestic industrial systems, which augmented the 'local content' in their production, and a larger number of minority shareholdings and takeovers of existing firms, whereas the previous trend had been greenfield investments with 100% Japanese ownership; (ii) a considerable increase both in the number of Japanese firms in Europe and in their R&D activities; (iii) a larger number of productive sectors receiving direct Japanese investments.

Bearing the overall pattern of these changes in mind — although, as shown by Figure 4.8, they do not affect all the European countries to an equal extent — it is of interest to analyse some of the principal features of Japanese participation in the industrial systems of the European countries in the mid-1990s. As in the case of the American multinationals, account will be taken of the sectoral distribution by country of both manufacturing activities and R&D activities.

As regards manufacturing, Tables 4.8 and 4.9 respectively display the comparative and absolute advantages of 11 European countries for location by Japanese firms in 16 of the production sectors covered by the JETRO survey.[11] The reference variable used in construction of these tables was the number of Japanese firms present in sector i of country j. Obviously, this measure is much more imprecise than the number of employees used in the case of the American multinationals, but it is the only one currently available.[12]

As in the case of the American multinationals, the location of Japanese firms is apparently determined by two different factors: (i) the competitive advantages of the Japanese firms themselves;

---

[11] The original figures were for 19 manufacturing sectors and 18 countries. However, to ensure a satisfactory level of significance in the estimates of the comparative and absolute advantages set out in the two tables, I have preferred to omit those countries or sectors with fewer than 10 Japanese firms. The sectors excluded (furniture, paper, iron and steel) have been aggregated under the heading 'other manufacturing industries'. The number of Japanese firms in the countries omitted from Tables 4.8 and 4.9 has nevertheless been included in the calculation of the absolute and comparative advantages of the other countries.

[12] Regarding the construction of the tables, comparative advantages (RLA) were calculated using the formula: $RLA = (N_{ij}/\sum_j N_{ij})/(\sum_i N_{ij}/\sum_i \sum_j N_{ij})$, where $N$ is the number of Japanese firms. Absolute advantages were instead represented by the percentage of Japanese firms in sector i of country j compared with the total number of Japanese firms operating in the same sector Europe-wide.

Table 4.8   Comparative Advantages of European Countries in the Location of Japanese Firms, 1994

| | UK (205) | France (111) | Germany (107) | Spain (86) | Holland (48) | Italy (47) | Belgium (41) | Ireland (33) | Portugal (14) | Austria (13) | Sweden (11) |
|---|---|---|---|---|---|---|---|---|---|---|---|
| Food (30) | 0.47 | 3.89 | 0.67 | 0.36 | 1.50 | 0.00 | 0.59 | 0.00 | 0.00 | 0.00 | 0.00 |
| Textiles (16) | 0.88 | 0.81 | 0.42 | 0.68 | 0.00 | 2.87 | 0.00 | 2.73 | 6.43 | 3.46 | 0.00 |
| Apparel and textile products (20) | 1.05 | 0.65 | 0.34 | 1.09 | 0.00 | 6.89 | 0.00 | 0.00 | 0.00 | 0.00 | 0.00 |
| Chemicals n.e.c. (127) | 0.94 | 0.97 | 0.69 | 0.94 | 1.77 | 0.84 | 1.66 | 0.69 | 0.81 | 0.87 | 1.03 |
| Pharmaceuticals (20) | 0.00 | 0.97 | 1.35 | 2.73 | 0.75 | 0.77 | 1.76 | 4.36 | 0.00 | 0.00 | 0.00 |
| Rubber goods (13) | 0.54 | 2.00 | 1.04 | 0.84 | 1.15 | 1.18 | 1.35 | 0.00 | 0.00 | 0.00 | 0.00 |
| Ceramics, stone and clay (17) | 0.62 | 0.38 | 1.19 | 1.28 | 0.88 | 0.00 | 5.16 | 2.57 | 0.00 | 0.00 | 0.00 |
| Nonferrous metals (12) | 0.59 | 2.16 | 0.56 | 0.00 | 0.00 | 1.28 | 0.00 | 1.82 | 8.57 | 0.00 | 0.00 |
| Metals products (33) | 1.17 | 0.39 | 0.82 | 1.65 | 0.91 | 1.39 | 0.53 | 0.66 | 0.00 | 6.71 | 0.00 |
| General machinery (87) | 0.85 | 0.75 | 1.70 | 0.88 | 1.21 | 1.23 | 0.81 | 0.50 | 0.00 | 0.64 | 2.26 |
| Electronic and electrical equipment (113) | 1.34 | 1.32 | 1.25 | 0.77 | 0.13 | 0.81 | 0.78 | 0.77 | 0.00 | 0.49 | 0.00 |
| Electronic components (61) | 1.38 | 0.43 | 1.43 | 0.54 | 0.98 | 0.00 | 0.58 | 3.58 | 0.00 | 0.00 | 1.07 |
| Transport equipment (19) | 0.74 | 0.68 | 0.00 | 3.44 | 0.79 | 2.42 | 0.92 | 0.00 | 2.71 | 0.00 | 0.00 |
| Transport equipment parts (53) | 1.39 | 0.61 | 0.51 | 1.65 | 0.85 | 0.87 | 0.66 | 0.00 | 2.91 | 1.04 | 2.47 |
| Precision instruments (37) | 1.04 | 1.05 | 1.82 | 0.00 | 1.22 | 0.00 | 0.47 | 0.00 | 0.00 | 1.50 | 3.54 |
| Others (62) | 0.85 | 0.63 | 0.54 | 1.06 | 1.45 | 0.74 | 1.13 | 1.06 | 3.32 | 1.79 | 1.06 |

*Notes*: The figure in brackets is the number of Japanese firms operating in the sector Europe-wide.
*Source*: My calculations on data from JETRO (1995).

Table 4.9 Geographical and Sectoral Distribution of Japanese Firms in Europe, 1994 (% Firms per Country in the Industry Total)

| | UK | France | Germany | Spain | Holland | Italy | Belgium | Ireland | Portugal | Austria | Sweden |
|---|---|---|---|---|---|---|---|---|---|---|---|
| Food (30) | 13.33 | 60.00 | 10.00 | 3.33 | 10.00 | 0.00 | 3.33 | 0.00 | 0.00 | 0.00 | 0.00 |
| Textiles (16) | 25.00 | 12.50 | 6.25 | 6.25 | 0.00 | 18.75 | 0.00 | 12.50 | 12.50 | 6.25 | 0.00 |
| Apparel and textile products (20) | 30.00 | 10.00 | 5.00 | 10.00 | 0.00 | 45.00 | 0.00 | 0.00 | 0.00 | 0.00 | 0.00 |
| Chemicals n.e.c. (127) | 26.77 | 14.96 | 10.24 | 8.66 | 11.81 | 5.51 | 9.45 | 3.15 | 1.57 | 1.57 | 1.57 |
| Pharmaceuticals (20) | 0.00 | 15.00 | 20.00 | 25.00 | 5.00 | 5.00 | 10.00 | 20.00 | 0.00 | 0.00 | 0.00 |
| Rubber goods (13) | 15.38 | 30.77 | 15.38 | 7.69 | 7.69 | 7.69 | 7.69 | 0.00 | 0.00 | 0.00 | 0.00 |
| Ceramics, stone and clay (17) | 17.65 | 5.88 | 17.65 | 11.76 | 5.88 | 0.00 | 29.41 | 11.76 | 0.00 | 0.00 | 0.00 |
| Nonferrous metals (12) | 16.67 | 33.33 | 8.33 | 0.00 | 0.00 | 8.33 | 0.00 | 8.33 | 16.67 | 0.00 | 0.00 |
| Metals products (33) | 33.33 | 6.06 | 12.12 | 15.15 | 6.06 | 9.09 | 3.03 | 3.03 | 0.00 | 12.12 | 0.00 |
| General machinery (87) | 24.14 | 11.49 | 25.29 | 8.05 | 8.05 | 8.05 | 4.60 | 2.30 | 0.00 | 1.15 | 3.45 |
| Electronic and electrical equipment (113) | 38.05 | 20.35 | 18.58 | 7.08 | 0.88 | 5.31 | 4.42 | 3.54 | 0.00 | 0.88 | 0.00 |
| Electronic components (61) | 39.34 | 6.56 | 21.31 | 4.92 | 6.56 | 0.00 | 3.28 | 16.39 | 0.00 | 0.00 | 1.64 |
| Transport equipment (19) | 21.05 | 10.53 | 0.00 | 31.58 | 5.26 | 15.79 | 5.26 | 0.00 | 5.26 | 0.00 | 0.00 |
| Transport equipment parts (53) | 39.62 | 9.43 | 7.55 | 15.09 | 5.66 | 5.66 | 3.77 | 0.00 | 5.66 | 1.89 | 3.77 |
| Precision instruments (37) | 29.73 | 16.22 | 27.03 | 0.00 | 8.11 | 0.00 | 2.70 | 0.00 | 0.00 | 2.70 | 5.41 |
| Others (62) | 24.19 | 9.68 | 8.06 | 9.68 | 9.68 | 4.84 | 6.45 | 4.84 | 6.45 | 3.23 | 1.61 |
| Total | 28.47 | 15.42 | 14.86 | 9.17 | 6.67 | 6.53 | 5.69 | 4.58 | 1.94 | 1.81 | 1.53 |

*Notes:* The totals per row are less than 100 because account was also taken of the Japanese firms operating in other European countries when constructing the table.

*Source:* My calculations on data from JETRO (1995).

(ii) the competitive advantages of the national production systems of countries receiving Japanese FDI. However, compared with the locational patterns of American firms in Europe, marked differences emerge in geographical and sectoral distribution, not least because of the diverse structure of the competitive advantages enjoyed by Japanese and American firms.

Great Britain seems to be the country in which the sectoral distribution of Japanese firms most closely reflects their competitive advantages. Flanking the comparative advantages offered by Great Britain for location by Japanese firms in the sectors of components for motor vehicles, electronic components, and electrical and electronic apparatus (Table 4.8), is the strong attraction exerted by British industry in the transport sector (Table 4.9). One notes the total absence of Japanese firms from the British pharmaceutical sector, although this is marked by the major presence of American and European firms seeking to exploit the British pharmaceutical industry's considerable technological assets in the area of biotechnologies (Cantwell, 1987, 1992b; Cantwell and Sanna Randaccio, 1992). Nonetheless, Japanese pharmaceutical firms have indeed closely involved themselves in British industry, but not by establishing production plants. In fact, although there is no Japanese firm operating in the British pharmaceutical industry, there are six fully independent (i.e. unconnected with any manufacturing plant) Japanese research centres in Great Britain (JETRO, 1995).

Turning to France and Germany, the Japanese desire to exploit the local technological base is even more apparent in these countries than in the case of Great Britain. As regards Germany, for example, its comparative and absolute advantages for leading sectors of Japanese industry (electrical and electronic apparatus, electronic components) are matched by the large number of Japanese firms in industries with a strong local technological tradition (machinery, precision instruments). For Germany too, Tables 4.8 and 4.9 display an apparent anomaly: despite the strength of the German car industry, no Japanese firm operates in this sector. Once again, however, one notes the presence of eight Japanese R&D centres in the car and car components sectors.

The low cost of Spanish labour seems to offer evident locational advantages to firms operating in scale-intensive sectors like motor vehicles and their components, metal materials and goods, and in traditional sectors like clothing. Apparently contrasting with the general pattern is the large number of Japanese pharmaceutical companies operating in Spain. However, one also notes the total lack of R&D activities, which is indicative of the scant technological content characterising the involvement of Japanese pharmaceutical firms in Spanish industry. The Spanish motor vehicles sector warrants specific examination. Indeed, although this sector of Spanish industry attracts more than 30% of the Japanese firms producing motor vehicles in Europe, these firms are specialised in motorbikes, commercial vehicles and off-road vehicles, whereas the bulk of Japanese car production in Europe is concentrated in Great Britain.[13]

As far as Italy is concerned, the most significant finding is the concentration of Japanese firms in the 'made in Italy' sectors — textiles and clothing[14] — and in sectors such as machinery, where the competitiveness of Italian firms is rapidly improving. As other authors have noted (e.g. Molteni, 1994; Ramazzotti, 1995), this is a distinctive feature of Japanese firms operating in Italian industry, which seem intent on acquiring its competitive advantages, amongst other things by purchasing minority shareholdings in domestic firms.

Some information on the technological content of the activities of Japanese multinationals can be obtained — given the lack of other meaningful data — from the distribution of Japanese R&D centres. This distribution can be plotted both with reference to Figure 4.8, discussed above, and on the basis of Figure 4.9, which shows the frequency of Japanese R&D centres in five macro-regions comprising 14 of the 15 countries currently belonging to the European Union.[15] As this figure shows very clearly, Japanese firms display a trend similar to the one noted previously when discussing American multinationals: as one moves from the centre to the periphery of Europe, technological activity diminishes considerably.

It is also of considerable interest to analyse the distribution of Japanese R&D centres per country and sector of economic activity. Table 4.10 shows the sectors of economic activity with

---

[13] The same applies to the Japanese firms producing motor vehicles in Italy.

[14] Note that multinationals from other countries are almost entirely absent from these sectors (cf. Chapter 6).

[15] The figures for Austria are not given, since this country cannot be included in any of the macro-regions considered. Austria has eight Japanese firms with R&D centres (73%) but no independent research centres.

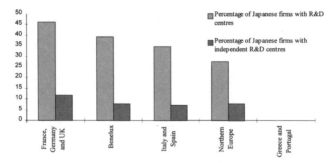

**Figure 4.9** Relative Intensities of Japanese R&D Centres in 5 European Macro-Regions, 1994
*Notes*: Benelux = Belgium, Holland and Luxembourg; Northern Europe = Finland, Norway, Sweden, Denmark and Ireland.
*Source*: My calculations on data from JETRO (1995).

Table 4.10   The Productive Sectors of the European Countries with the Highest Concentrations of Japanese Research Centres, 1994

| | | | |
|---|---|---|---|
| United Kingdom (97) | Electronics and telecommuni-cations (42) | Transport equipment [2] (11) | Machinery (10) |
| France (37) | Electronics and telecommuni-cations [3] (9) | Pharmaceu-ticals [1] (8) | Transport equipment [2] (6) |
| Germany (60) | Electronics and telecommuni-cations [3] (20) | Machinery (12) | Pharmaceu-ticals [1] (8) Transport equipment [2] (8) |
| Spain (24) | Electronics and telecommuni-cations [3] (6) | Chemicals (6) | Transport equipment [2] (5) |
| Italy (15) | Machinery (8) | Clothing (2) | Chemicals (2) |

*Notes*: The figure in brackets denotes the number of R&D centres.
[1] Including the cosmetics industry, with 5 R&D centres in France and 2 in Germany.
[2] Including parts and components for motor vehicles.
[3] Including electronic components.

the strongest concentrations of Japanese R&D centres in the five leading countries of the European Union. Analysis apparently confirms the previous finding on the distribution of Japanese firms among the industries of the European countries. Whereas in the majority of the latter, R&D activities are concentrated in sectors with very marked competitive advantages by Japanese firms, primarily electronics and telecommunications, in Italy the match between the competitive advantages of national industry and Japanese R&D activity is more pronounced, as demonstrated by the concentration of Japanese R&D centres in the machinery and clothing sectors.

It appears, however, that the Japanese desire to exploit local scientific and technological assets also influences — albeit to a lesser extent in the Italian case — the location of R&D activities in the other European countries. This is evidenced by the large number of Japanese R&D centres in the machinery, pharmaceuticals and motor vehicles sectors in Germany, and in the pharmaceuticals (cosmetics) and motor vehicles sectors in France.


## 4.6. CONCLUSIONS

The large amount of empirical evidence set out in previous pages suggests various further lines of inquiry in specification of the factors that determine the attractiveness of the various European countries for investments by foreign MNEs, and in explanation of the differing behaviour of American and Japanese firms in Europe. Leaving to the interested reader the task of exploring the various aspects of the involvement of American and Japanese firms in Europe, also on the basis of the information provided in this chapter, in these conclusions I shall restrict my discussion to the empirical evidence that has emerged most clearly.

First, the technological content of the activities conducted by American and Japanese firms in Europe differs considerably among the countries belonging to the European Union. Germany and Great Britain alone attract more than half of the productive and innovative activities of American and Japanese multinationals in Europe. Italy, Spain, Greece and Portugal jointly account for only 10%, in terms of the same variables.

However, the figures on the innovative and productive activity of the European subsidiaries of American and Japanese multinationals show that these indicators vary considerably among productive sectors. This finding is to some extent at odds with the aggregate classifications, and it is indicative of the pronounced specialisation of the passive internationalisation of the countries of Western Europe. Indeed, the sectoral distribution of direct American and Japanese FDI seemingly replicates both the strengths and weaknesses of the industrial systems of the European countries, and also those of the investor countries.

The variability of the involvement of American firms in European industries is heightened by the marked differences that emerge in the role played by their subsidiaries in the creation of technology. Whereas those American subsidiaries that operate in countries with longer-established and/or more developed systems seem largely to satisfy their technological requirements on their own, in the other countries they rely principally on technology imported from the parent-company, probably targeting their modest amount of R&D activity on adaptation of their technologies to the requirements of local markets. By contrast, technological sourcing activity by Japanese firms in Europe, in the leading sectors of national productive and innovative systems, seems to be high even in countries like Italy characterised by the low presence of multinationals.

One gains the impression that the reallocation of productive and innovative activities by American and Japanese multinational firms tends to reproduce and perpetuate the disequilibria among the Western European countries. However, detailed analysis of the overall effects of the passive internationalisation of the European economies must necessarily take account of the influence exerted by the presence of foreign multinationals on domestic firms. This topic will be analysed in the next two chapters, which focus on Great Britain (Chapter 5) and on Italy (Chapter 6).

# 5. Foreign Multinationals and Domestic Firms: Empirical Evidence for the United Kingdom

## 5.1. INTRODUCTION

During the 1980s, as in previous decades, the United Kingdom attracted a much larger share of FDI than did the other European countries. Thanks to an industrial policy which did not discriminate against foreign firms, to vigorous action taken by the state to curb trade-union power,[1] and to the incentives provided for new FDI in the depressed areas of the country, Great Britain managed to consolidate its traditional locational advantages for European investments made by MNEs from every part of the world.

FDI assumed great importance for the strategies of industrial development pursued by the Conservative governments of the period. However, rather than adding extra impetus to the industrial development of the country, such investment only hastened the decline of British industry's competitiveness. In other words, although the economy made great strides in the reorganisation of economic activity in favour of the banking and financial sector, the fate of the manufacturing industry was almost entirely entrusted to the entry of foreign firms able to relieve or replace by now poorly competitive domestic firms,

---

[1] At the end of the 1980s the cost of labour in British industry had reached one of the lowest levels among the most developed countries of Western Europe. Ireland, Greece and Portugal were the only countries in the EEC and EFTA that offered cheaper labour (Ray, 1990).

and to rejuvenate the country's industrial system by injecting new and competitive technological knowledge and managerial expertise.

Having largely abandoned hope of reviving important national industries like cars and domestic appliances, governments and economists turned their attention to less ambitious goals, such as the possible positive effects of the presence of foreign MNEs on vertically linked local firms. That is to say, although in important industrial branches little or nothing could be done to save competitive domestic firms, FDI could help those vertically connected to the productive networks of foreign MNEs, thus stimulating the exchange of technologies and managerial skills. This was reflected in mounting concern over the fact that the limited competitiveness of domestic firms, and their unwillingness to change their productive and managerial methods, might hamper the growth of beneficial vertical relations between foreign and local firms, especially in the case of new Japanese investment (Dunning, 1986; Strange, 1993).

Despite substantial changes in the overall role assigned to FDI in British industry, ever since the 1950s the presence of foreign MNEs had been of fundamental importance for the country. Depending on the circumstances, it had either boosted or braked the productive and technological development of national industry. As a consequence, a large body of literature arose which offered, however, conflicting solutions. For example, as early as the late 1950s Dunning had highlighted the importance of competitive stimuli, and of technological flows between local firms and American multinationals, for the increased competitiveness of British industry (Dunning, 1958). Almost three decades later he argued with some important distinctions for the positive effects exerted by the presence of the foreign affiliates of Japanese MNEs on the competitiveness of British suppliers and competitors (Dunning, 1986). Similar conclusions concerning Japanese investments during the 1980s were reached by Brech and Sharp (1984), who also emphasised the importance of the 'demonstration' effects on domestic firms of the productive and managerial methods employed by Japanese firms. But much more pessimistic forecasts were made by Young, Hood and Hamill (1988), who contended that the foreign presence would be only *"a modest palliative"* for the competitiveness of British industry. Oliver and Wilkinson

(1988) went even further, claiming that if radical changes were not made to industrial policy (especially as regards the financing of firms), *"...the Japanisation of British manufacturing industry...will be at the expense of British-owned companies, and a further decline in the quality, if not quantity of Britain's manufacturing base."*[2]

These general conclusions should not, of course, be allowed to obscure the differing impact of the foreign presence on Britain's various productive sectors. The cases of the British automobile and pharmaceutical industries have been frequently cited as examples of, respectively, the vicious and virtuous circles generated by the foreign presence (Cantwell, 1987; Cantwell and Dunning, 1991). As repeatedly pointed out in previous chapters, these studies assert the existence of a close link between the initial technological competence of domestic firms and the effects of the foreign presence on the development of local industry.

On the other hand, whatever its effects may have been, the foreign presence in British industry during the 1980s is of great interest to those setting out to analyse the implications of the growing internationalisation of productive activities for the industrial and technological development of European industry. Indeed, the combination in this period of decidedly *laissez-faire* policies in the internal market and great openness to international investment meant that Great Britain is an ideal case for assessment of the effects of FDI. Without any form of state intervention via industrial policy (except for the tax relief and benefits granted to foreign firms investing in depressed areas of the country), the British case enables projections to be made of the future effects of uncontrolled worldwide competition between national and multinational firms.

## 5.2. THE CHARACTERISTICS AND CONSEQUENCES OF THE FOREIGN PRESENCE IN BRITISH INDUSTRY

Table 5.1 shows foreign penetration in British manufacturing industry between 1981 and 1991 in terms of employees, sales

---

[2] Oliver and Wilkinson (1988, p. 173).

Table 5.1  Foreign Penetration in Terms of Employees, Sales, Output, Value Added and Investments. Great Britain, Manufacturing Industry, 1981–1991

| Year | Employment % | Sales % | Net output % | Value added % | Investment % |
|------|------|------|------|------|------|
| 1981 | 14.85 | 19.41 | 18.55 | 18.30 | 25.55 |
| 1983 | 14.49 | 20.37 | 18.97 | 18.61 | 23.05 |
| 1984 | 14.15 | 20.56 | 19.49 | 19.30 | 20.39 |
| 1985 | 13.98 | 20.33 | 18.84 | 18.12 | 21.32 |
| 1986 | 12.73 | 18.95 | 17.34 | 16.96 | 19.69 |
| 1987 | 13.37 | 21.00 | 19.05 | 17.92 | 21.32 |
| 1988 | 12.87 | 20.13 | 18.07 | 17.77 | 20.77 |
| 1989 | 14.86 | 21.06 | 21.48 | 20.59 | 27.55 |
| 1990 | 16.01 | 25.00 | 22.28 | 21.67 | 26.86 |
| 1991 | 17.07 | 25.40 | 22.43 | 21.61 | 33.38 |

*Source*: *Business Monitor PA 1002*, various years.

volume, output, value added, and investments.[3] Whichever indicator is chosen, the pronounced increase in the foreign presence from the early 1990s onwards is obvious. During the 1980s, penetration in terms of employees oscillates around 13–15%, while penetration in terms of sales, output, value added and investments is invariably higher, and continues to be so in the 1990s. The gap between penetration in terms of employees and penetration in terms of sales, output and value added evidences the greater labour productivity achieved in aggregate by the subsidiaries of foreign MNEs compared with domestic firms. Which is probably partly explained by the greater investments per employee made by the former, as shown by comparison between the first and last columns of Table 5.1. One also notes the difference between penetration in terms of sales on the one hand, and in terms of output and value added on the other, where the ratio is always in favour of the former indicator. This suggests that some foreign firms only import finished products and components to assemble, which are then sold after minor alterations on European markets.

---

[3] As already pointed out in the previous chapter, the British figures refer only to majority shareholdings.

Foreign penetration in British industry varies considerably from one manufacturing sector to another. Table 5.2 sets out the figures on foreign penetration in terms of employees and output in the 18 manufacturing sectors to which reference will be made henceforth. The years considered are 1983 and 1989. It was deemed advisable not to extend the analysis to subsequent years in order not to admix the effects of the international recession in the early 1990s.[4]

Foreign penetration was very marked in sectors with high technological content: office machinery, for example, where almost half the national industry was controlled by foreign companies,[5] and the chemicals industry, as well as scale sectors like car production. Still at modest levels were traditional sectors like textiles, footwear and clothing, and the timber and furniture industry.

A first question to address on the basis of these figures is the stability or otherwise of the structural characteristics of the foreign penetration in British industry. To this end a 'Galtonian regression' was carried out, assuming foreign penetration in 1989 ($FOR_{1989}$) as the dependent variable and foreign penetration in 1983 ($FOR_{1983}$) as the independent variable:

$$FOR_{i,1989} = \alpha + \beta FOR_{i,1983} \qquad (5.1)$$

where the subscript $i$ denotes the productive sector.

The appendix gives technical details on this type of regression. Here, I point out that values of $\beta > 1$ indicate that over time foreign firms tend to increase their presence in those sectors in which they are already highly specialised. Instead, when $\beta$ is less than 1, this is a case of 'regression towards the mean' and the foreign presence tends to distribute itself uniformly among the industrial sectors. If $0 < \beta < 1$, the industrial sectors tend to maintain their position in the league table of foreign presence, but are closer to each other. If $\beta < 0$, the table tends be reversed, and the specialisation pattern is stood on its head.

---

[4] Already in 1990 Great Britain's rate of growth of GDP had fallen from 2.3% in the previous year to 1%.

[5] This percentage increased greatly in 1990, when foreign shareholding in the office machinery sector reached 53.87% in terms of employees and 74.29% in terms of output.

Table 5.2   Foreign Penetration in 18 Manufacturing Sectors, Great Britain, 1983 and 1989

| ISIC REV. 2 | Sector | Employment | | Net output | |
|---|---|---|---|---|---|
| | | 1983 | 1989 | 1983 | 1989 |
| 22 | Metal manufacturing | 13.34 | 17.99 | 16.78 | 16.85 |
| 24 | Manufacturing of non metallic mineral products | 6.57 | 9.83 | 7.19 | 10.20 |
| 25 | Chemical industry | 32.89 | 32.11 | 36.56 | 35.31 |
| 26 | Production of man made fibres | 9.84 | 12.24 | 15.46 | 16.50 |
| 31 | Manufacture of metal goods not elsewhere specified | 8.32 | 8.25 | 10.99 | 11.63 |
| 32 | Mechanical engineering | 19.30 | 16.99 | 23.28 | 21.94 |
| 33 | Manufacturing of office machinery and data processing equipment | 31.59 | 48.39 | 31.44 | 48.13 |
| 34 | Electrical and electronic engineering | 16.23 | 17.87 | 18.60 | 20.15 |
| 35 | Manufacture of motor vehicles and other parts thereof | 36.04 | 35.98 | 45.12 | 52.18 |
| 36 | Manufacture of other transport equipment | 1.94 | 3.63 | 2.09 | 3.48 |
| 37 | Instrument engineering | 23.15 | 20.46 | 25.31 | 23.01 |
| 41/42 | Food, drink and tobacco | 11.77 | 10.90 | 16.46 | 19.35 |
| 43 | Textile | 2.98 | 4.13 | 3.72 | 6.19 |
| 45 | Footwear and clothing | 3.46 | 2.69 | 5.16 | 4.75 |
| 46 | Timber and wooden furniture | 2.03 | 2.84 | 2.85 | 4.32 |
| 47 | Paper and paper products; printing and publishing | 14.39 | 14.09 | 16.79 | 19.16 |
| 48 | Processing of rubber and plastic | 21.06 | 19.05 | 24.09 | 24.34 |
| 49 | Other manufacturing industries | 15.30 | 8.11 | 20.59 | 9.57 |

*Source: Business Monitor PA 1002*, various years.

Moreover, if $|\beta| > |R|$, where $R$ is the square root of the coefficient of correlation, the variance of the *FOR* variable is greater at the end rather than at the beginning of the period considered, which indicates that the productive specialisation of foreign firms increases over time. The opposite is the case when $|\beta| < |R|$.

Table 5.3 gives the results obtained with reference to penetration in terms of both employees (variable *FORE*) and net output (*FORNO*). As well as the usual statistics, the square roots of the coefficient of correlation, $R$, are given. In both cases, coefficient $\beta$ is positive and not significantly different from 1 (*t*-statistics not shown), while the absolute value of $\beta$ is greater than $R$. This suggests that the pattern of industrial penetration by foreign firms in 1983 has consolidated further over time. In sectors where such penetration was relatively greater, foreign firms have acquired larger shares of the British market, compared with those sectors in which foreign penetration was relatively modest at the beginning of the period.

Having analysed the principal structural features of the foreign penetration in British industry, we may now turn our attention to the performance of foreign firms compared with domestic ones in terms of factor productivity. Since reliable estimates of the capital stock of the two groups of firms are not available, the following analysis will be based solely on the productivity of labour defined in terms of value added per employee.

Table 5.3 The Stability of the Specialisation Pattern of Foreign Penetration, Great Britain, 1983–1989

| Dependent variable | $\alpha$ | $\beta$ | $\bar{R}^2$ | $R$ |
|---|---|---|---|---|
| $FORE_{1989}$ | −0.002 | 1.071 | 0.85 | 0.93 |
| | (−0.155) | (7.900)*** | | |
| $FORNO_{1989}$ | −0.289 | 1.092 | 0.86 | 0.93 |
| | (0.246) | (11.152)*** | | |

*Notes*: The symbols *, ** and *** indicate that the coefficients are significantly different from zero at the 90%, 95% and 99% level of probability (two-tail test). The standard errors have been corrected for the heteroscedasticity of the residues using the procedure described by White (1980). *t*-statistics in brackets.

Table 5.4   The Productivity of Domestic and Foreign Firms, Great Britain, 1983 and 1989

|  | $GAP_{1983}$ | $GAP_{1989}$ | $DGAP\%$ | $DPROD\%$ |
|---|---|---|---|---|
| Foreign firms |  |  |  | 39.08 |
| Domestic firms | 1.35 | 1.52 | 12.00 | 24.17 |

*Notes*: The *GAP* variable is the ratio between value added per employee in foreign firms and value added per employee in domestic ones. *DPROD%* and *DGAP%* denote respectively the percentage growth of productivity and the productivity gap between the two groups of firms. Productivity growth in the two groups was obtained after deflating the variables for the industrial production price index. The figures given in the table are those for the set of 18 manufacturing sectors listed in Table 5.2.

Table 5.4 sets out significant indices of the comparative performances of the two groups of firms. In the period considered, both groups achieved considered growth in labour productivity; but the gap to the disadvantage of domestic firms, which amounted to 38% in 1983, continued to widen until it reached 52% in 1989. It should be stressed that although part of the competitive advantage of foreign firms may derive from their larger size compared with the average of their local competitors, as Hughes (1993) has shown, this factor alone cannot account entirely for the productivity gap between them.[6]

The aggregate figures given in Table 5.4 of course conceal important differences at the level of individual production sectors. But these differences do not substantially alter the fact that there was a wide and generalised gap between domestic and foreign firms in terms of labour productivity. In fact, in both 1983 and 1989 only in very few production sectors did domestic firms register a productivity gap slightly in their favour,[7] while in others, like cars, the food industry, artificial fibres and clothing, the productivity gap was more than 50% in 1989.

---

[6] Hughes has shown that between 1983 and 1987 productivity growth in foreign firms was 24.5%, as opposed to the 16.9% of domestic firms and the 1.7% of domestic firms with more than 200 employees. The hypothesis formulated by Hughes (1993) to obtain this result was that all the firms with fewer than 200 employees were domestic.

[7] The office machinery sector in 1983 and the manufacturing sectors of metal products, office machinery and other means of transport equipment in 1989.

A general picture of changes in the competitiveness gap between domestic and foreign firms in the period 1983–89 can be obtained by once again using a Galtonian regression, which in this case is specified as:

$$GAP_{i,1989} = \alpha + \beta \, GAP_{i,1983}. \qquad (5.2)$$

Table 5.5 summarises the results. $\beta$ is positive and significantly different from 0 and less than 1 (although in this case the difference is not significant), and it is also less than the square root of the coefficient of correlation. This signifies that the structure of sectoral differences in terms of labour productivity remained relatively stable over time. The sectors in which the technological gap was most accentuated did not greatly improve their relative positions, and the same applies to those in which the gap was less pronounced. Moreover, intersectoral differences grew more marked, as shown by the increase in the intersectoral variance of the gap in terms of labour productivity ($|\beta| > |R|$).

These findings apparently confirm Cantwell's (1989) predictions discussed in detail in previous chapters. When the initial technological competence of domestic firms is higher — that is, in the foregoing analysis, in the sectors where the initial productivity gap is slight — domestic firms can more easily exploit the positive externalities arising from the foreign presence in national industry. Conversely, in sectors where local industry is initially more backward compared with foreign competitors — that is, those in which the productivity gap is wider — foreign competition displaces local firms, which are caught up in a vicious circle of declining competitiveness. Consequently, as shown by the Galtonian regressions discussed above, a given structure of relative competitiveness

Table 5.5 The Stability of the Productivity Gap Between Domestic and Foreign Firms, Great Britain, 1983–1989

| Dependent variable | $\alpha$ | $\beta$ | $\bar{R}^2$ | $R$ |
|---|---|---|---|---|
| $GAP_{1989}$ | 0.357 | 0.753 | 0.25 | 0.54 |
| | (1.031) | (2.562)** | | |

*Notes*: See Table 5.3.

of domestic industrial sectors compared to foreign competitors tends to consolidate over time, due to the foreign presence, thereby accentuating the strengths and weaknesses of national industry.

Before passing to more formal analysis of these hypotheses, discussion is required of the data given in Table 5.6., which apparently confirm the above findings while adding further useful information. These figures were obtained by dividing the sample of 18 sectors into four sub-samples according to whether the initial technological gap and foreign presence in 1983 was above or below the average. This yielded the respective sub-samples of *HIGHGAP*, *LOWGAP*, *HIGHFORE* and *LOW-FORE*, which were then aggregated.

Domestic firms achieved the worst performance in sectors where a substantial initial foreign presence corresponded to a wide gap in terms of the productivity of the factors. By contrast, disparities in terms of relative competitiveness prevented domestic firms from catching up with the affiliates of foreign MNEs to a much lesser extent in sectors with a low foreign presence and/or lower initial technological gap.

Although these results should be treated with the necessary caution, they seem to confirm the conclusions reached in Chapter 3 on the basis of numerical simulations. As then pointed out, the amount of technological spillovers depends, *ceteris paribus*, on two main factors: technological disparities and the level of foreign presence. In combination, these two factors

Table 5.6  Percentage Variations in the Productivity Gap Between Domestic and Foreign Firms in Four Macro-Sectors, Great Britain, 1983–1989

|  | *HIGHFORE* | *LOWFORE* | **Total** |
|---|---|---|---|
| *HIGHGAP* | 36.67 | 14.22 | 29.09 |
| *LOWGAP* | 5.59 | 7.28 | 3.54 |
| Total | 13.00 | 9.53 | 12.00 |

*Notes*: The figures correspond to the percentage variations of the gap between foreign and domestic firms in terms of labour productivity between 1983 and 1989. They refer to the 18 manufacturing sectors listed in Table 5.2.

determine the relative competitiveness of domestic firms, and therefore the profit level and the resources available for imitation of foreign technologies and the pursuit of local lines of technological development — and also, obviously, the resources available for new plant and machinery. Wide technological gaps can therefore be more easily closed when the foreign presence is modest and in slow growth, rather than when technologically backward domestic firms must cope with strong competitive pressure by foreign firms on the national territory.

## 5.3. TECHNOLOGICAL SPILLOVERS AND TECHNOLOGICAL COMPETENCE: AN EMPIRICAL VERIFICATION

The theoretical model proposed in Chapter 3 suggests the following stylised facts:

1. The average productivity growth of domestic firms stimulated by the presence of foreign MNEs on the national territory may be broken down into two distinct but interrelated phenomena:
   a. the processes of industrial selection which expel less efficient firms from the market
   b. technological spillovers.
2. The amount of possible spillovers is positively correlated with the degree of technological competence possessed by domestic firms. However, industries with low or very low levels of development can in some cases benefit from the higher level of economic activity associated with FDI.
3. By rapidly eroding the profits realised by domestic firms, and therefore the resources available for R&D activities, strong and/or rapidly growing foreign penetration may reduce the ability of domestic firms to close the technological gap.

The pages that follow set out empirical evidence useful for verification of the validity of the model in question on the basis of the statistics available for Great Britain for the years 1983 and 1989. The analysis refers to the 18 manufacturing sectors already discussed.

*Test 1: Technological Competence and Productivity Growth*

The first hypothesis tested was the relation between the productivity growth of domestic firms and the initial technological gap, defined as the ratio between the labour productivity in the subsidiaries of foreign MNEs and in domestic firms in each production sector. For each of the equations estimated, labour productivity was expressed in terms of both value added per employee and of net output per employee.

A first attempt to estimate a linear relation between productivity growth in domestic firms and initial technological gap yielded disappointing results (low coefficient of determination and non-significance of the independent variable). This, however, was not surprising in the light of the discussion in Chapter 3. Industries in which the initial technological competence of domestic firms is particularly developed benefit from intense technological spillovers which generate virtuous circles of development. The reverse process characterises sectors with average technological development, where foreign technological superiority leads to the displacement of local industry unable to appropriate foreign technology. In industries with low or extremely low levels of technological development, local firms can at least benefit from the expansionary effects associated with a greater foreign presence and, perhaps, from the birth of vertical relations between domestic firms and subsidiaries of foreign MNEs.[8]

Consequently, an estimate was made of a quadratic relation between the two variables, taking the form:

$$DVAED_{83-89,i} = a_0 + a_1\, GAPVAE_{83,i}$$

$$+ a_2\, GAPVAE^2_{83-89,i} + \varepsilon_t, \qquad (5.3)$$

or alternatively:

$$DNOED_{83-89,i} = a_0 + a_1\, GAPNOE_{83,i}$$

$$+ a_2\, GAPNOE^2_{83-89,i} + \varepsilon_t, \qquad (5.4)$$

---

[8] One notes that the high degree of aggregation of the industrial sectors used for the empirical analysis means that in many cases vertically linked firms can be included in the same production sector.

where $DVAED_{83-89}$ and $DNOED_{83-89}$ respectively represent the percentage growth of labour productivity in domestic firms between 1983 and 1989 in terms of value added and output per employee,[9] while $GAPVAE_{83}$ and $GAPNOE_{83}$ denote the initial productivity gap in terms of the same variables. In both cases, in the light of the arguments set out above, the predicted value of the coefficient $a_2$ is positive.

The results in the first two rows of Table 5.7 seemingly confirm the above assertion concerning the varying effects of the foreign presence according to the initial technological gap. Both the equations estimated give good results in terms of the variance explained. Moreover, in both cases the coefficient $a_2$ assumes the sign expected. However, although satisfactory, these estimates are liable to be influenced by a few anomalous data, given the low number of observations made. Graphic inspection of the figures suggests that there are only three sectors in which a wide initial technological gap is associated with its reduction in the period 1983–1989. Consequently, the estimates were reiterated on the basis of a linear relation after these sectors were eliminated: namely, 'manufacturing of metal goods', 'man-made fibres' and 'other manufacturing industries'. Their anomalous behaviour (wide initial technological gap but strong growth of productivity in domestic firms and simultaneous narrowing of the technological gap) may be explained — apart from the existence of a non-linear relation which ties the performance of domestic firms to the initial technological gap — by the particular features of these sectors. In fact, the heterogeneity of the sector 'other manufacturing industries' may by itself account for the anomalous performance of domestic industries. In the case of the 'man-made fibres' sector, its small size may give rise — following the failure of a few domestic firms or their purchase by foreign firms — to marked variations in average productivity in the two groups of firms.[10] Finally, as regards the 'manufacturing of metal goods' sector, the non-complexity of the technologies used in this sector may generate major spillovers even in the presence of a wide initial technological gap.

---

[9] All the variables relative to the productivity and output of domestic and foreign firms used for the empirical analysis in this section have been deflated for the industrial production price index (*Source*: OECD).
[10] In 1983 this sector accounted for only 0.2% of total output by manufacturing industry, and it comprised only four foreign firms.

Table 5.7   Productivity Growth of Domestic Firms and Initial Technological Gap, Great Britain, OLS Estimates, 1983–1989

(a) $DVAED_{83-89}$ = 2.609   − 3.730 $GAPVAE_{83}$ + 1.439 $GAPVAE^2_{83}$   $\bar{R}^2 = 0.56$   $n = 18$
            (4.028)***   (4.138)***   (4.917)***

(b) $DNOED_{83-89}$ = 4.511   − 6.620 $GAPNOE_{83}$ + 2.538 $GAPNOE^2_{83}$   $\bar{R}^2 = 0.29$   $n = 18$
            (3.199)***   (3.002)***   (2.989)***

(c) $DVAED_{83-89}$ = 0.562   − 0.285 $GAPVAE_{83}$   $\bar{R}^2 = 0.15$   $n = 15$
            (2.526)**   (−1.550)

(d) $DNOED_{83-89}$ = 0.689   − 0.363 $GAPNOE_{83}$   $\bar{R}^2 = 0.30$   $n = 15$
            (3.773)***   (2.471)**

*Notes*: The symbols *, ** and *** indicate the significance of the coefficients at the 90%, 95% and 99% level of probability (two-tail test). The values of the Student's *t*-test given in brackets were obtained after correcting the standard errors for the heteroscedasticity of the residues using the procedure described by White (1980).

The results obtained for the remaining 15 sectors are given in the last two rows of Table 5.7.

The explanatory capacity of the equations is considerably reduced when value added per employee is used as the measure for labour productivity, while it remains substantially unchanged when net output per employee is employed. However, both equations seem to confirm the importance of initial technological capacity for the performance achieved by domestic firms in the period considered.

### Test 2: Technological Competence and Catching-up

More than productivity growth in domestic firms, it appears important to measure their performance compared with the subsidiaries of foreign MNEs operating in the country. For this reason, analysis follows of the dynamics of the technological gap.

In the light of the results discussed in the previous section, a first attempt was made using a quadratic specification:

$$DGAPVAE_{83-89,i} = a_0 + a_1 \, GAPVAE_{83,i}$$
$$+ a_2 \, GAPVAE^2_{83-89,i} + \varepsilon_t \qquad (5.5)$$

and

$$DGAPNOE_{83-89,i} = a_0 + a_1 \, GAPNOE_{83,i}$$
$$+ a_2 \, GAPNOE^2_{83-89,i} + \varepsilon_t, \qquad (5.6)$$

where $DGAPVAE_{83-89}$ and $DGAPNOE_{83-89}$ represent the percentage growth of the technological gap between 1983 and 1989. In contrast to the previous section, here $a_2 < 0$ is predicted. In fact, if the above hypotheses are valid, the technological gap will tend to diminish in sectors where the initial gap in relative competitiveness between domestic and foreign firms is small, and also in sectors where the technological and productive development of local firms is so modest that only positive externalities are possible. Conversely, in sectors lying midway between these two extremes cases, the displacement effects will tend to prevail over technological spillovers.

It should also be pointed out that the parameters estimated in these regressions are significant only after one sector ('manufacturing of metal goods') has been eliminated.

As in the previous section, the equations were re-estimated on the basis of a linear relation, after the three sectors listed above had been eliminated (equations (g) and (h) in Table 5.8). In both cases, the dependent variable proved to be positively correlated with the initial technological gap. In sectors where domestic firms are technologically more backward, the technological gap tends to widen over time; *vice versa* in those where the initial technological competence of domestic firms is relatively high.

## *Test 3: Firm's Size and Absorption Capacity*

A third group of estimates were carried out by dividing the sample of domestic firms between those of small (fewer than 100 employees) and medium-large size. In effecting this division, it was necessary to introduce the hypothesis that the group of firms with fewer than 100 employees consisted only of domestic firms. Since estimates of value added for the firms with fewer than 100 employees are not given separately, reference will be made to output per employee alone.

If the sample is broken down in this manner, the explanatory capacity of the estimated model increases considerably in the case of firms of medium-large size, whereas it is slightly reduced for small firms with respect to equation (h). The results obtained are set out in Table 5.9 (equations (i) and (j)), where the variables DGAPNOES and DGAPNOEML denote the percentage variation of the technological gap in small and medium-large firms respectively.

Also of particular interest are the results reported in the bottom row of Table 5.9. We saw in Chapter 3 that the extent of the FDI flow may be an important determinant of the reactive capacity of domestic firms, especially the weakest of them. Given the unavailability of data on FDI at a level of disaggregation adopted bythe present analysis, the growth of net output by foreign firms ($DNOF_{83-89}$) was used as a proxy for this variable, which proved to be positively correlated with the growth of the

Table 5.8 The Dynamics of the Technological Gap, OLS Estimates, Great Britain, 1983–1989

(e) $DGAPVAE_{83-89}$ = $-2.011$ + $3.090\ GAPVAE_{83}$ $-$ $1.125\ GAPVAE^2_{82}$   $\bar{R}^2 = 0.20$   $n = 17$
    $(2.488)^{**}$   $(2.754)^{**}$   $(3.158)^{***}$

(f) $DGAPNOE_{83-89}$ = $-3.457$ + $5.305\ GAPNOE_{83}$ $-$ $1.963\ GAPNOE^2_{83}$   $\bar{R}^2 = 0.15$   $n = 17$
    $(2.542)^{**}$   $(2.609)^{**}$   $(2.634)^{**}$

(g) $DGAPVAE_{83-89}$ = $-0.553$ + $0.517\ GAPVAE_{83}$   $\bar{R}^2 = 0.36$   $n = 15$
    $(3.100)^{***}$   $(3.381)^{***}$

(h) $DGAPNOE_{83-89}$ = $-0.616$ + $0.562\ GAPNOE_{83}$   $\bar{R}^2 = 0.51$   $n = 15$
    $(4.001)^{***}$   $(4.535)^{***}$

*Notes:* As for Table 5.7.

Table 5.9 Small and Medium-Sized Firms and Foreign Presence, OLS Estimates, Great Britain, 1983–1989

(i) $DGAPNOES_{83-89}$ = $-0.295$ + $0.338\ GAPNOES_{83}$   $\bar{R}^2 = 0.24$   $n = 15$
    $(2.377)^{**}$   $(3.723)^{***}$

(j) $DGAPNOEML_{83-89}$ = $-0.827$ + $0.730\ GAPNOEML_{83}$   $\bar{R}^2 = 0.66$   $n = 15$
    $(5.915)^{***}$   $(6.458)^{***}$

(k) $DGAPNOES_{83-89}$ = $-0.439$ + $0.388\ GAPNOES_{83}$ + $0.176\ DNOF_{83-89}$   $\bar{R}^2 = 0.37$   $n = 15$
    $(3.323)^{***}$   $(4.489)^{***}$   $(2.437)^{**}$

*Notes:* As for Table 5.7.

technological gap in the case of smaller firms (equation k), although a significant correlation was not found in the case of medium-large ones. Moreover, in the case of small firms, the explanatory capacity of this new regression proved to be considerably greater than that of the previous one (equation (i)).

This result is not surprising in the light of the earlier discussion. It is plausible, in fact, that small firms are less able to mobilise the financial resources necessary to cope with a rapid increase in foreign penetration.

## Test 4: Industrial Selection and Foreign Presence

The data available are not sufficient for detailed analysis of the interaction between the foreign presence and selection processes at the sectoral level. The only statistical relation that sheds some light on this phenomenon is between the output growth of domestic firms and the initial technological gap.

Where the process of industrial selection is not important, there should be no significant relation between these variables: the technological gap does not affect the market shares of individual domestic firms. Instead, where industrial selection is marked, the relation should be negative: a wide technological gap exerts a negative influence on market shares and therefore on output by domestic firms.

The results set out in Table 5.10 seem to support the later hypothesis. With regard to the initial gap in terms of both output and value added per employee, the technological gap apparently hampers the capacity for expansion of domestic firms measured by their percentage growth of output ($DNOD_{83-98}$).

Table 5.10   Growth of Output and Technological Gap, OLS Estimates, Great Britain, 1983–1989

| | | | | |
|---|---|---|---|---|
| (l)  $DNOD_{83-89}$ | $= 0.655$ | $- 0.349\ GAPVAE_{83}$ | $\bar{R}^2 = 0.22$ | $n = 15$ |
| | $(4.152)^{***}$ | $(2.850)^{**}$ | | |
| (m)  $DNOD_{83-89}$ | $= 0.750$ | $- 0.417\ GAPNOE_{83}$ | $\bar{R}^2 = 0.34$ | $n = 15$ |
| | $(5.087)^{***}$ | $(3.711)^{***}$ | | |

*Notes*: As for Table 5.7.

## 5.4. CONCLUSIONS

The presence of foreign MNEs in British industry seems to be a factor that triggers virtuous and vicious circles in its development. The analysis conducted in this chapter has evidenced the link between the technological competence of domestic industry and the ability of the production system to withstand the challenges raised by the internationalisation of production. Both the capacity of domestic firms to increase their productivity at a rate comparable with that achieved by foreign firms, and their growth of output, are negatively correlated with the initial level of the technological gap between domestic and foreign firms. However, this gap plays a much more modest role in sectors which use relatively simple and standardised technologies.

In keeping with the conclusions reached in Chapter 3, the impact of the foreign presence on the performance of local firms is particularly harmful in sectors where a wide technological gap is accompanied by high foreign penetration. In this case, the competitive pressure associated with FDI considerably reduces the profitability of domestic firms. In all likelihood it therefore also reduces their investment in new plant, machinery and R&D, which is inevitably to the detriment of their prospects for development.

The lesson to be learnt from the British case seems to be, once again, that it is necessary to control the level of foreign presence and to ensure that the rate of expansion of FDI is commensurate with the level of technological competence reached by the domestic industrial system. If domestic industry lags technologically far behind its foreign competitors, policies of pronounced openness to foreign productive capital may greatly reduce those positive effects which direct foreign investment is able to generate under other conditions. *Laissez-faire* policies *vis-à-vis* the internationalisation of production are therefore, in many cases, not the best solution available to the industrialised countries: they tend to accentuate the weaknesses of national industrial systems, and they are apparently unable to revive the fortunes of industries in severe competitive decline.

## APPENDIX

### *The Galtonian Regression*

The Galtonian regression technique originated in biology (Galton, 1889) and was subsequently applied in economic analysis by, among others, Hart and Prais (1956), Hart (1976) and Cantwell (1989).

With reference to Eq. (A.5.1) the technique consists in OLS estimation of $Y_{i,t}$ on $Y_{i,t-1}$:

$$Y_{i,t} = \alpha + \beta Y_{i,t-1} + \varepsilon_{i,t} \quad \text{for } i = 1, \ldots, n. \qquad (A.5.1)$$

The standard hypothesis is that $\varepsilon_{i,t}$ is normally distributed, stochastic and independent of $Y_{i,t-1}$.

If $Y$ is taken to measure the foreign presence, $\beta > 1$, as represented by line (1) in Figure A.5.1, then the classification table of sectors in terms of foreign presence at time $t$ tends to be the same as at time $t-1$. The case of $\beta < 1$ is instead that of a 'regression towards the mean' represented by line (3), where the foreign presence tends to distribute itself uniformly among the sectors. If $0 < \beta < 1$, industries tend to remain in the same place in the classification, but they are closer to each other. If $\beta < 0$, the classification is completely inverted.

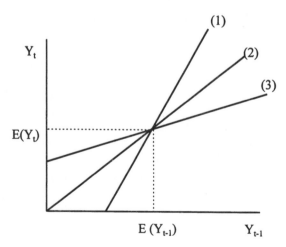

**Figure A.5.1**   The Galtonian Regression

Comparison between the absolute values of $R$ and $\beta$ from Eq. (A.5.1) yields

$$\sigma_t^2 = \beta^2 \sigma_{t-1}^2 + \sigma_\varepsilon^2. \qquad (A.5.2)$$

Since

$$R^2 = 1 - (\sigma_\varepsilon^2/\sigma_t^2) = (\sigma_t^2 - \sigma_\varepsilon^2)(1/\sigma_t^2), \qquad (A.5.3)$$

by combining (A.5.2) and (A.5.3) we have

$$\sigma_t - \sigma_\varepsilon^2 = \beta^2 \sigma_{t-1}^2 = R^2 \sigma_t^2 \qquad (A.5.4)$$

and therefore

$$\sigma_t^2/\sigma_{t-1}^2 = \beta^2/R^2. \qquad (A.5.5)$$

Consequently, if $\beta^2 > R^2$, i.e. if $|\beta| > |R|$, then $\sigma_t^2 > \sigma_{t-1}^2$.

# 6. The Characteristics and Consequences of the Foreign Presence in Italian Industry

## 6.1. INTRODUCTION

In recent years, amongst other things because of the greater amount of statistics available, the theme of FDI in Italian industry has been the subject of a growing number of studies. Although different aspects of the phenomenon have been investigated, the possible consequences of the foreign presence on the competitiveness of Italian firms — meaning by this term firms controlled by Italian industrial groups or entrepreneurs — has only been marginally addressed by economic analysis.

Study of the causes and effects of FDI in Italy interweaves closely with the features of the national industrial system and with the country's industrial policy choices (or non-choices). The structure of the competitive advantages of Italian industry hinges on a close-knit system — though one confined to a limited area of the national territory — of small and medium-sized firms in specialised and traditional sectors. This means that the conditions under which the encounter (or clash) between international production and the domestic innovative and productive system comes about are, in many respects, unique. The question arises in particular as to whether the specific features of Italian industry enable it to react positively to the challenges raised by the growing internationalisation of production activities or whether, instead, they impede Italian industry from seizing the opportunities provided by the more intense international mobility of production capital and of technological knowledge. In this context, the lack of any industrial policy designed to attract FDI[1] and distribute it among the developed and depressed areas of the country, as well as the absence of any measure to foster the exchange of technologies and managerial expertise between domestic and foreign firms, raise further questions as to the ability of Italian industry to cope with the passive internationalisation of the economy.

My aim in this chapter is to suggest an interpretation of these phenomena. Without claiming to provide an exhaustive account, I shall seek, first, to analyse the features of the foreign presence in Italian industry, highlighting as far as possible the differences between Italian and foreign firms in each production sector in terms of the productivity of the factors and of openness to exchanges with abroad. Second, by specifying a cross-sectional econometric model, I shall attempt to assess the impact of the foreign presence on labour productivity in Italian firms.

The chapter is organised as follows. Section 6.2 provides a brief description of the problems arising from the productive internationalisation of Italian industry relative to the structural characteristics of the country's industrial system. Section 6.3 analyses the differences in terms of performance between Italian firms and foreign MNEs as far as labour productivity and the percentage of exports on total sales are concerned. Section 6.4 sets out an econometric analysis of the impact of the foreign presence on the dispersion of labour productivity internally to individual production sectors. Section 6.5 draws some conclusions.

## 6.2. THE FOREIGN PRESENCE IN ITALIAN INDUSTRY: A SUMMARY

Foreign penetration is certainly not a novelty for the Italian industrial system. After the Second World War, American

---

[1] Strange (1993) points out that Italy is the only country of Western Europe without an agency set up to promote direct foreign investments in domestic industry, and the only country which does not produce promotional literature.

direct investments in Italian industry were probably a major factor in the country's industrial take-off, equipping the Italian economy with the capital and technologies that it required to catch up with the more industrialised countries (Cainarca, 1992; Piscitello, 1994). In those years, the Italy's low level of industrial development meant that every foreign investment gave an *additional* boost to economic growth, without questions being raised as to the possible displacement effects of competition by American firms on nascent national industry.

Today, the importance of FDI is particularly evident when account is taken of the overall degree of internationalisation (i.e. the direct investments both entering and leaving the country) of the Italian economy, and its strengths and weaknesses. Firstly, the structural weakness of the Italian industrial system in high-tech sectors is matched by a strong presence of foreign firms in these same sectors. This circumstance can be explained by the small size of Italian science-based sectors, and by the propensity of foreign firms to invest in these sectors rather than others.[2] Secondly, the degree of productive internationalisation of domestic firms is markedly lower in all those sectors in which the process is most advanced in the other industrialised countries (Mariotti, 1988; Cominotti and Mariotti, various years). It should also be stressed that the pronounced sectoral and geographical heterogeneity of Italian industrial development suggests that the capacity of Italian firms to withstand competition by foreign MNEs varies considerably among production sectors and geographical areas. And this augments the virtuous and vicious circles generated by inward FDI.

Figure 6.1 provides an overview of the degree of internationalisation of Italian industry in relation to inward and outward FDI flows at the end of 1991; information which will be useful for more detailed analysis of the topics presented above.[3] The figure has been constructed on the basis of the

---

[2] For example, in 1991 whereas nationally only 9% of the total workforce of manufacturing firms was employed in science-based sectors, around 24% of the employees of foreign firms were concentrated in these sectors, when only majority shareholdings are considered, and around 27% when minority shareholdings are also included in the calculation.

[3] There is a slight discrepancy between the figures published in Cominotti and Mariotti (1992) and those set out by Figure 6.1 and Table 6.1 in the next section on direct foreign investment. This is due to the constant updating of the *Ricerche e Progetti* data base. The figures used here are updated to December 1994.

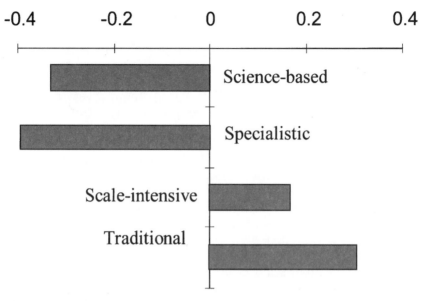

**Figure 6.1**   The Productive Internationalisation of Italian Industry (Normalised Balances), 1991
*Source*: My elaboration of *Ricerche e Progetti* data.

normalised balances between inward and outward FDI per employee obtained using the formula:

(employees in foreign firms with Italian shareholding
  − employees in Italian firms with foreign shareholding)/
(employees in foreign firms with Italian shareholding
  + employees in Italian firms with foreign shareholding)

In both science-based and specialised sectors one notes a considerable disproportion between inward and outward FDI, to the detriment of the latter. In science-based sectors the low internationalisation level of Italian firms is the direct result of the weakness of the national industrial system in high-tech sectors. The prevalence of inward over outward FDI, moreover, evidences the potential role of this form of internationalisation as the source of technological knowledge acquired from foreign competitors. The case of specialised sectors is more complex. The competitive advantages of Italian industry do not seem to be matched by comparable penetration by Italian firms of foreign markets. The weakness deriving from the small size of domestic industry, which prevents its more pronounced internationalisation (Mariotti, 1992), is accompanied by the growing interest of foreign MNEs in the technological advantages of Italian firms, which gives rise to a conspicuous amount of inward investment.[4] Moreover, a convincing explanation of the limited internationalisation of Italian industry in specialised sectors may be the fact that the increased competitiveness of the Italian producers of capital goods is a relatively recent phenomenon, dating to the mid-1980s (Balloni, 1995). Consequently, a certain amount of time will have to pass before its effects become manifest in terms of FDI flows.[5] It is likewise probable that the structural features of the competitive advantages of Italian firms, which stem largely from the country's system of industrial districts, provide scant stimulus for their productive internationalisation (Kogut and Zander, 1993).

The scale-intensive sectors are those in which inward and outward FDI most closely approaches parity. In this case, as discussed in more detail in the next section, the weaknesses and strengths of Italian firms compared with their foreign competitors exhibit an alternating pattern. Contrasting with sectors in which the technological backwardness of national industry is flanked by a large foreign presence and a low level of internationalisation of Italian firms — chemicals, for instance — are sectors like domestic appliances, car components and rubber goods in which the quantity of inward and outward FDI testifies to the dynamism of the Italian industrial system (Cominotti and Mariotti, various years).

---

[4] This trend is evidenced by the behaviour of Japanese investors in Italy, who seem to prefer minority shareholding in Italian firms operating in sectors where they enjoy solid competitive advantages (machinery, chemicals, textiles, clothing, and motor vehicle components), rather than in those sectors (car manufacture and domestic appliances) in which Japanese firms have built their own competitive advantages and which principally attract their investments in other European countries (Molteni, 1994). For further details on direct Japanese investment in Italian industry see Chapter 4.

[5] The available data show that this process is already under way. Between 1985 and 1993, whilst employees in Italian firms with foreign shareholding operating in the specialised sectors grew by little more than 4%, those working for foreign firms with Italian shareholding in the same sectors increased by more than 200% (Cominotti and Mariotti, 1994). This latter increase did not show signs of faltering even during the recent international recession.

Finally, in traditional sectors — with the exception of the food industry, where the globalisation of productive activity is more marked — the competitive advantage of Italian firms seems to thwart the penetration of foreign firms. The latter, in fact, seem to prefer the opportunities offered by the Asiatic export-processing zones, rather than sustain the costs of gaining access to Italy's more competitive productive structure.

This overview of the internationalisation of Italian industry raises numerous questions concerning the relationship between inward and outward FDI and technological development: in particular, the ability of Italian firms to respond to the increased competitive pressure deriving from the internationalisation of productive activities by rapidly absorbing the technological capabilities of foreign competitors — being helped to do so by the physical proximity of the two groups of firms, Italian and foreign — and their ability to defend their competitive advantages against increased technological sourcing activities by the foreign MNEs operating in the country.

## 6.3. THE PERFORMANCE OF DOMESTIC AND FOREIGN FIRMS IN ITALIAN INDUSTRY

The two principal sources of statistics for the empirical analysis conducted in this and the next section are the *Ricerche e Progetti* Reprint data bank on FDI in the Italian industry (Cominotti and Mariotti, various years) and the *Mediocredito Centrale* survey of small and medium-sized manufacturing firms (Mediocredito Centrale, 1994).

The former of these two sources comprises information on the sales and the number of employees of foreign firms operating in Italy for the period 1983–1993. It was used to construct the indices of penetration by foreign firms in Italian industrial sectors.

The second source contains firm-level data gathered by questionnaires periodically administered by *Mediocredito Centrale* and provides information of various kinds — sales, employees, exports, R&D activity, etc. — for the years 1989–1991. This information was used to highlight the distinctive characteristics of domestic and foreign firms operating in the country, and to construct the variables used in the econometric analysis in the next section.

Of the 4811 firms surveyed by *Mediocredito Centrale*, 426 declared that they were owned a foreign group.[6] Assuming that the *Ricerche e Progetti* survey is complete as regards foreign firms operating in Italy, these represent 35.3% of the resident firms controlled by foreign companies or groups. However, incompleteness or other anomalies in the statistics meant that the sample had to be reduced to 4042 firms (391 of which were foreign).[7]

The relative brevity of the time-period considered by the *Mediocredito Centrale* survey counselled against conducting dynamic analysis.

Table 6.1 gives an overview of the performances of two groups of firms. To facilitate consultation of the figures, the firms have been grouped into macro-sectors *à la* Pavitt.[8]

The first column shows the gap in terms of labour productivity expressed by the ratio between value added per employee in foreign firms and Italian firms. Despite a certain amount of variability and anomalies displayed by this indicator internally to the macro-sectors *à la* Pavitt, the general picture that emerges seemingly confirms the well-known strengths and weaknesses of Italian industry.

The science-based sectors display a wider gap, especially in the information technology and office machinery sector, and substantial equality of performance by domestic and foreign

---

[6] It should be pointed out that the notion of 'membership of a group' adopted by *Mediocredito Centrale* is that of art. 2359 of the Civil Code, which refers both to control exercised through possession (direct or through an intermediary company or person) of the majority vote at the ordinary general meeting of shareholders, or at any rate a block of votes such that it has a dominant influence, and to dominant influence exercised by virtue of particular contractual provisions. Since the definition of a controlled firm used by *Ricerche e Progetti* (50% plus 1 of votes) is much more restricted than that contained in the civil code, any direct comparison between the two statistical sources is purely indicative.

[7] 670 firms were eliminated because their balance-sheet figures (value added, sales volume, plant and machinery) were not available, 88 because they operated in non-manufacturing sectors, 8 because they could not be classified as belonging to a 3-digit sector, and 3 because they operated in sectors in which no foreign firms were present, according to the *Ricerche e Progetti* data (sectors 120 and 429, respectively coke-making and tobacco).

[8] The classification *à la* Pavitt (Pavitt, 1984) adopted by *Mediocredito Centrale* is slightly different from that used by Cominotti and Mariotti (various years) to analyse the foreign presence in Italy. To ensure greater comparability with previous studies on direct foreign investment in Italy, a classification similar to Cominotti and Mariottis has been used in this book.

Table 6.1   Foreign Penetration and the Relative Performance of Italian and Foreign Firms, 1991

| | Relative performance | | Foreign penetration % |
|---|---|---|---|
| | Value added per employee | Exports/ Sales | |
| Chemicals derivatives | 1.59 | 0.89 | 49.07 |
| Pharmaceuticals | 0.98 | 3.00 | 57.47 |
| Office machinery and information technology | 4.72 | 1.64 | 79.77 |
| Electronics and telecommunications | 1.15 | 2.08 | 61.86 |
| Aircraft | n.a. | n.a. | 0.78 |
| **Science-based sectors** | **1.58** | **1.80** | **51.29** |
| Plant and machinery | 0.94 | 0.65 | 18.09 |
| Electromechanical | 0.99 | 0.84 | 24.62 |
| Precision machinery | 1.22 | 0.33 | 20.51 |
| **Specialist sectors** | **0.97** | **0.66** | **19.90** |
| Refined petroleum products | 1.16 | 1.49 | 27.45 |
| Primary metal products | 1.04 | 1.81 | 7.64 |
| Non-metallic minerals | 1.05 | 1.25 | 8.09 |
| Glass | 1.15 | 2.00 | 21.96 |
| Base chemicals | 1.06 | 1.19 | 28.62 |
| Consumer chemicals products | 2.01 | 0.23 | 85.07 |
| Artificial and synthetic fibres | n.a. | n.a. | 14.92 |
| Metal products | 1.29 | 0.13 | 5.70 |
| Electrical cables | 1.64 | 1.14 | 21.79 |
| Electrical components and products | 1.12 | 1.85 | 29.80 |
| Domestic appliances | 1.09 | 2.18 | 39.77 |
| Motor vehicles and bodywork | 1.44 | 13.77 | 3.50 |
| Components for motor vehicles | 0.78 | 1.04 | 39.72 |
| Other transport equipment | 1.18 | 1.74 | 3.79 |
| Derived foodstuffs | 0.78 | 3.56 | 33.59 |
| Beverages | 0.96 | 2.18 | 41.79 |
| Paper | 1.17 | 1.48 | 20.01 |

Table 6.1 (*Continued*)

| | Relative performance | | Foreign penetration % |
|---|---|---|---|
| | Value added per employee | Exports/ Sales | |
| Tyres and rubber products | 1.07 | 2.38 | 36.54 |
| Plastic products | 0.87 | 1.73 | 12.15 |
| **Scale-intensive sectors** | **1.19** | **1.27** | **17.19** |
| Basic foodstuffs | 0.89 | 1.27 | 10.36 |
| Textiles | 0.80 | 1.92 | 3.58 |
| Clothing and leather goods | 1.33 | 1.32 | 1.27 |
| Timber and furniture | 1.14 | 1.92 | 1.21 |
| Printing and publishing | 1.04 | 0.26 | 13.75 |
| Other manufacturing industries | 2.60 | 0.68 | 6.32 |
| **Traditional sectors** | **1.03** | **1.19** | **4.38** |
| Total | 1.30 | 1.10 | 17.15 |

*Notes*: n.a. = not available. The figure on total foreign penetration refers to the 33 production sectors listed in the table and described in greater detail in the appendix.
*Source*: My calculations on data from Mediocredito Centrale, Ricerche e Progetti and ISTAT.

firms in the pharmaceuticals sector.[9] Among the macro-sectors *à la* Pavitt, the specialist sectors are those in which Italian firms perform best compared with their foreign counterparts. Confirmed in particular is the well-known competitiveness of Italian industry in the plant and machinery sector. The scale-intensive group of sectors exhibits greater heterogeneity in terms of the relative competitiveness of Italian and foreign

---

[9] A possible explanation for the performance of the two groups of firms in the latter sector is the considerable discrepancies among national regulations concerning the pharmaceuticals industry. This circumstance, which creates substantial extra costs in adapting products to local markets, may have reduced the impact on productivity by the competitive advantages of large multinational groups as regards technological capacity.

firms. Whereas the strength of the former lies in sectors associated with the food industry, plastics and components for motor vehicles, the latter achieve a better performance in consumer chemical products, electrical cables, and motor vehicles and bodywork.[10] In all the other scale-intensive sectors, and as regards the macro-sector as a whole, there are no significant differences between Italian and foreign firms in terms of labour productivity. In traditional sectors, confirmation is provided of the strength of Italian industry in textiles and foodstuffs, although there is a wide productivity gap in the 'other manufactures' sector. Apparently anomalous is the performance of Italian firms in the clothing sector, where foreign firms record higher labour productivity than do their Italian competitors; a finding which may indicate the concentration of the (few) foreign firms operating in this sector on productions with relatively high value added.[11]

Also interesting are the relative performances of foreign and Italian firms in terms of the share of sales destined for exports. The second column of Table 6.1 sets out the ratio between the values assumed by this variable in the two groups of firms. Such comparison is important because it indicates the type of FDI made in Italian industry; and it is especially useful for assessment of whether this investment is made in order to serve the Italian market or the broader European one.

A first comparison among the four macro-sectors *à la* Pavitt shows that foreign firms are more export-oriented than their Italian counterparts in the science-based, scale-intensive and traditional sectors, although the difference is very marked in the first of these sectors and less so in the other two. Entirely the opposite pattern emerges in the specialist sectors, where domestic firms are much more oriented to foreign markets.

The function of FDI in Italian industry as an 'export platform' is very evident in the sectors of motor vehicles and bodywork, derived foodstuffs, pharmaceuticals, tyres and rubber products, domestic appliances, beverages, and electronics and telecommunications. More generally, one notes the greater propensity to

---

[10] For many of the scale-intensive and traditional sectors, however, the small number of Italian and foreign firms in the *Mediocredito Centrale* data basis reduces the significance of the comparison. See Table A.6.2. in the appendix.

[11] See the empirical evidence proposed in Chapter 4 concerning Japanese direct foreign investment in Italian industry.

export of foreign firms compared with Italian ones in almost all the sectors examined, with the exception of specialist sectors, consumer chemical products, chemical derivates, metal products, publishing and printing, and other manufactures.

Finally, column 3 of Table 6.1 lists the figures on foreign penetration in terms of employees, taking account of both minority and majority shareholdings. Here Italian industry displays marked heterogeneity as regards inward FDI. The science-based sectors, with the exception of the aerospace sector, are largely controlled by foreign MNEs.[12] To the extent, indeed, that to the well-known weakness of Italian industry in these sectors, as highlighted by analyses of foreign trade or technological indicators, should be added the fact that foreign investors are responsible for a large proportion of Italian industry's scant activity in these sectors. Among the macro-sectors *à la* Pavitt there follow in order of importance in terms of foreign penetration the specialist sector, the scale-intensive sector, and then, lagging behind with only 4.38% of employees in firms with foreign shareholding, the traditional sectors. One notes in these last two macro-sectors the high level of foreign presence in consumer chemical products, in tyres and rubber products, in domestic appliances, in components for motor vehicles, and in foodstuffs as a whole.

## 6.4. FOREIGN PENETRATION AND
## THE TECHNICAL EFFICIENCY OF ITALIAN FIRMS

As discussed in detail in previous chapters, the concept of 'technological spillovers' is generally associated with a positive effect exerted by the presence of foreign MNEs on the competitiveness of local firms. However, the occurrence of negative externalities cannot be ruled out. The latter may arise when the market power of MNEs introduces a monopolistic bias into competition; or likewise when the purchase of a domestic firm by a foreign one breaks existing vertical links and therefore undermines the cohesion of the domestic productive and innovative system; or lastly when the greater competitive pressure resulting

---

[12] Regarding the amount of control exerted by foreign firms on the Italian industrial system, it should be borne in mind that more than 80% of foreign shareholdings in Italian industry are majority shareholdings (Cominotti and Mariotti, various years).

from FDI is such that the displacement effects on domestic firms are greater than the positive externalities.

The empirical evidence shows that besides yielding higher rates of labour productivity growth in domestic firms (Caves, 1974; Globerman, 1979; Blomstrom and Persson, 1983; Kokko, 1992), the presence of technological spillovers helps domestic firms to more closely approach the best performing firm in terms of labour productivity in each sector (Blomstrom, 1989).

However, measurement of so-called technological or productivity spillovers is not without its difficulties. First, the view that the reduced dispersion of productivity is a consequence of inward FDI, if proven, does not explain whether this is due to the fact that local firms have moved closer to the domestic technological frontier or to their assimilation of technologies used in the plants of their foreign competitors (Haddad and Harrison, 1993). Second, the lesser dispersion of labour productivity may be due to the fact that less competitive firms have been forced out of the market. Moreover, it is not clear what proportion of the technological capabilities of individual firms or a sectoral aggregation of them can be explained by differences in terms of factor productivity.

The first of these problems can be partly obviated by the analysis conducted in the following pages. By comparing the dispersion of labour productivity among all firms (Italian and foreign) in the same sector, and then among Italian firms alone, it is possible to verify whether the foreign presence enables domestic firms to achieve levels of productivity comparable with those of foreign firms, or whether it favours aggregation around the domestic technological frontier. However, it is more difficult to give an exhaustive answer to the other two questions, although, as far as the ability of productivity indices adequately to represent the technological level (or at any rate a firm's degree of competitiveness) is concerned, the generally close match between the labour productivities of Italian and foreign firms on the one hand, and the strengths and weaknesses of Italian industry on the other, suggests such a close correlation between these two variables to justify the use of productivity indicators alone.[13]

---

[13] As well as these problems, which specifically relate to the type of econometric analysis conducted in the pages that follow, there is a perhaps even greater difficulty concerning all cross-sector analyses of technological spillovers: in the search for significant correlations between the foreign presence in each industrial sector and the

The methodology employed in this section closely follows that used by Haddad and Harrison to analyse the impact of the foreign presence on the dispersion of productivity in a large sample of Moroccan firms. Once productivity in each firm $i$ of sector $j$ has been calculated, the firm with the best performance in each sector is identified, and the percentage difference between the productivity of the factors in the $i$-th firm and the so-called 'best practice technique' of the sector is calculated:

$$\hat{a}_{ij} = VA_{ij}/L_{ij}, \qquad (6.1)$$

$$\hat{a}_j = \max(\hat{a}_{ij}), \qquad (6.2)$$

$$\hat{u}_{ij} = (\hat{a}_j - \hat{a}_{ij})/\hat{a}_j, \qquad (6.3)$$

where $VA_{ij}$ indicates the value added and $L_{ij}$ the number of employees of firm $i$ operating in sector $j$.

The new variable $\hat{u}_{ij}$ thus obtained is then used as the dependent variable.[14] The independent variables are the degree of foreign penetration measured in terms of the percentage of workers employed in sector $j$ by foreign MNEs operating in Italy $(FOR_j)$, and also two variables designed to measure the amount of scale economies (expressed by the size of the firm in terms of employees) and the capital/labour ratio. Given that the latter two variables may differently affect the labour productivity of each firm in a sector, rather than their absolute value I have once again preferred to use the percentage difference between the value of the variable for the firm and its maximum value internally to each sector (thereby obtaining the new variables $DEVADD_{ij}$ and $DEVKL_{ij}$). Finally a binary dummy variable $(FIRM_{ij})$, which assumes a value equal to 1 if

---

productivity of domestic firms in the same sector the problem of how to measure technological spillovers is entirely overlooked. In the light of the existing interactions between small and medium-sized firms in traditional or scale-intensive sectors and their suppliers of capital goods (Balloni, 1995), this aspect may be of great importance when quantifying the effects of the foreign presence on Italian industry.

[14] In 2 of the 4 science-based sectors comprising foreign firms, the highest level of labour productivity is achieved by the latter. In specialist sectors the ratio is 1 to 3, in scale-intensive ones 2 to 18, and in traditional ones 1 to 6.

the firm belongs to a foreign group and 0 otherwise, has been included in the regressions which comprise both domestic and foreign firms. This was done in order to control for the existence of possible factor productivity advantages enjoyed by MNEs independently of firm's size and the intensity of the capital/labour ratio.

As regards the expected sign of the coefficients of the independent variables, this will in all probability vary according to the sector considered. Table 6.2 gives a summary of these expected signs (minus indicates that a higher value of the explanatory variable tends to reduce the dispersion of productivity).

In all sectors, but in scale-intensive ones especially, a negative correlation is predicted between the deviation of the productivity of each firm from the sectoral production frontier and the variables indicating firm's size and the intensity of the capital/labour ratio. It is more difficult to predict the sign of the *FIRM* and *FOR* variables. As regards the former, firms in science-based sectors can probably count on technological advantages which secure them higher labour productivity compared with domestic firms, intensity of the labour/capital and size remaining equal. However, since technological advantages sooner or later tend to translate into larger market shares, it is not clear what proportion of them can be explained by the *DEVADD* and *DEVKL* variables. In this connection, Haddad and Harrison (1993) report a positive correlation between total productivity of the factors and foreign ownership in Moroccan manufacturing sectors. By contrast, Globerman, Ries and Vertinsky (1994) do not discern any advantage enjoyed by foreign firms in terms of value added per employee in a sample of Canadian companies, once account has been taken of

Table 6.2    Expected Signs for the Coefficients of the Independent Variables

|  | *FOR* | *DEVADD* | *DEVKL* | *FIRM* |
|---|---|---|---|---|
| All sectors | ? | − | − | ? |
| Science-based | + | − | − | − |
| Specialist | − | − | − | ? |
| Scale-intensive | − | − | − | ? |
| Traditional | ? | − | − | ? |

differences in size and in the intensity of the capital/labour ratio. Finally, in the light of the foregoing discussion, it is likely that the sign of the *FOR* variable will vary among the macro-sectors *à la* Pavitt. In sectors where the technological competence of Italian firms is high (specialist and scale-intensive sectors), one would expect them to be able to mobilise the resources necessary to assimilate the productive externalities generated by the foreign presence. By contrast, when, as in the science-based sectors, a high foreign presence combines with wide technological disparities, the displacement effect on local firms associated with FDI may justify a positive sign for the coefficient of the *FOR* variable. Separate discussion is required of the traditional sectors, where, despite the well-known dynamism of small and medium-sized Italian firms, the modest presence of foreign firms (see Table 6.1) suggests that there are no significant relations between the latter and the dependent variable.

Table 6.3 illustrates the results obtained by OLS estimates on the entire sample of 4042 firms, both Italian and foreign. Although the foreign presence is negatively and significantly correlated with the dispersion of productivity in aggregate, it gives rise to conflicting results internally to the macro-sectors *à la* Pavitt. In the specialist and scale-intensive sectors, its coefficient is negative and significant. The reverse is the case in the science-based sectors, where a positive coefficient is obtained. In traditional sectors, no significant relations emerge between foreign presence and labour productivity at the firm level. The coefficients of the *DEVADD* and *DEVKL* variables always assume the expected sign, and in all cases they are statistically different from zero — apart from the science-based sectors, where the size variable is statistically null. Comparison among the absolute values of the coefficients of these variables in the macro-sectors shows that the bulk of the scale economies obtainable in scale-intensive and specialist sectors derive more from the differing intensity of the capital/labour ratio than from the number of employees. The coefficient of the binary *FIRM* variable is significant only in the case of specialist sectors, which may be due to the possible relation between competitiveness and market share discussed above.

The positive value assumed by the coefficient of the *FOR* variable in the science-based sectors, taking account of the competitive advantage apparently enjoyed by foreign firms in

Table 6.3   The Impact of the Foreign Presence on the Dispersion of Labour Productivity. Dependent Variable: Deviation from the Best Practice Technique ($\hat{u}_{ij}$). Italian and Foreign Firms

|  | All | Science-based | Sectors Specialistic | Scale-intensive | Traditional |
|---|---|---|---|---|---|
| Intercept | 0.861 | 0.631 | 1.404 | 0.840 | 0.853 |
|  | (202.725)*** | (14.286)*** | (40.206)*** | (114.735)*** | (140.802)*** |
| FOR | −0.001 | 0.003 | −0.026 | −0.001 | 0.001 |
|  | (5.278)*** | (4.245)*** | (14.336)*** | (2.337)** | (0.580) |
| DEVADD | −0.139 | −0.112 | −0.198 | −0.059 | −0.204 |
|  | (6.136)*** | (−1.246) | (2.938)*** | (2.143)** | (4.676)*** |
| DEVKL | −0.433 | −0.295 | −0.469 | −0.526 | −0.289 |
|  | (20.392)*** | (3.826)*** | (9.195)*** | (15.839)*** | (10.392)*** |
| FIRM | −0.009 | −0.021 | −0.033 | 0.002 | −0.013 |
|  | (0.980) | (0.805) | (1.847)* | (0.129) | (0.683) |
| $n$ | 4042 | 258 | 710 | 1758 | 1316 |
| $\bar{R}^2$ | 21.9 | 25.9 | 42.6 | 23.8 | 15.9 |

*Notes:* The symbols *, **, and *** indicate the significance of the coefficients at the 90%, 95% and 99% level of probability (two-tail test). The values of the student's t-test given in brackets were obtained after correcting the standard errors for the heteroscedasticity of the residues using the procedure described by White (1980).

these sectors, raises the problem of quantifying what proportion of the dispersion of productivity internally to these sectors is directly due to the entry of foreign firms, whose technological advantages are reflected in a higher index of productivity and therefore in a forward shift of the technological frontier, or to the displacement of local firms, or to other negative effects associated with FDI. One may also enquire, more in general, whether the effect of FDI is to move Italian firms closer to, or further from, the domestic technological frontier, or alternatively closer to or further from that of foreign firms.

Two further tables of OLS estimates may be useful in answering these questions. In Table 6.4 the estimates previously carried out have been repeated for Italian firms alone. Table 6.5 sets out the estimates obtained on the same sample of firms, but in this case the production frontier has been calculated with foreign firms excluded, thereby altering the dependent variable ($\tilde{u}_{ij}$).

With reference to the first columns of these two tables, the results do not seem to diverge from those obtained previously: neither the coefficients nor their level of significance change greatly. However, matters are different when one moves to analysis of the results for the macro-sectors.

In the science-based sectors, the *FOR* variable remains significant only when foreign firms are included in calculation of the production frontier. This suggests that the foreign presence is not important as far as the transfer of advanced foreign technologies is concerned; nor does it enable local firms to move closer to (or further away from) the domestic production frontier. In other words, the massive presence of foreign firms in Italy seems not to stimulate the development of a comparable domestic industry in the technologically more advanced sectors. If one adds to this finding the well-known weakness of Italian industry (comprising both Italian firms and a large number of subsidiaries of foreign MNEs) in terms of its competitiveness on international markets, a picture emerges which is even more pessimistic than that generally painted of the state of these sectors in Italy.[15]

---

[15] In other words, on the one hand Italy's performance in these sectors is poor, on the other it is largely due to the subsidiaries of foreign multinational firms, rather than to Italian firms, and strong foreign penetration does nothing to help domestic firms.

Table 6.4   The Impact of the Foreign Presence on the Dispersion of Labour Productivity. Dependent Variable: Deviation from the Best Practice Technique ($\hat{u}_{ij}$). Italian Firms

|  | All | Science-based | Sectors Specialistic | Scale-intensive | Traditional |
|---|---|---|---|---|---|
| Intercept | 0.864 | 0.636 | 1.380 | 0.840 | 0.851 |
|  | (202.247)*** | (16.265)*** | (38.614)*** | (109.018)*** | (144.943)*** |
| FOR | −0.001 | 0.003 | −0.025 | −0.001 | 0.001 |
|  | (4.812)*** | (4.783)*** | (13.340)*** | (1.911)* | (0.707) |
| DEVADD | −0.159 | −0.052 | −0.256 | −0.076 | −0.205 |
|  | (6.096)*** | (0.551) | (3.339)*** | (2.260)** | (4.656)*** |
| DEVKL | −0.444 | −0.385 | −0.456 | −0.534 | −0.283 |
|  | (20.846)*** | (6.786)*** | (8.835)*** | (14.773)*** | (11.116)*** |
| n | 3651 | 186 | 629 | 1565 | 1271 |
| $\bar{R}^2$ | 21.6 | 40.1 | 43.1 | 23.3 | 15.4 |

*Notes:*  As for Table 6.3.

Table 6.5 The Impact of the Foreign Presence on the Dispersion of Labour Productivity. Dependent Variable: Deviation from the Best Practice Technique ($\tilde{u}_{ij}$). Italian Firms

| | All | Science-based | Sectors Specialistic | Scale intensive | Traditional |
|---|---|---|---|---|---|
| Intercept | 0.859 | 0.773 | 1.425 | 0.832 | 0.849 |
| | (194.814)*** | (12.618)*** | (37.655)*** | (111.746)*** | (144.698)*** |
| FOR | −0.001 | 0.0001 | −0.027 | −0.001 | −0.001 |
| | (6.374)*** | (0.098) | (14.012)*** | (3.193)*** | (0.091) |
| DEVADD | −0.143 | 0.012 | −0.245 | −0.068 | −0.254 |
| | (5.789)*** | (0.139) | (3.219)*** | (2.146)** | (5.806)*** |
| DEVKL | −0.398 | −0.450 | −0.418 | −0.441 | −0.284 |
| | (19.084)*** | (5.807)*** | (7.998)*** | (12.644)*** | (11.261)*** |
| n | 3651 | 186 | 629 | 1565 | 1271 |
| $\bar{R}^2$ | 21.6 | 23.5 | 39.6 | 21.3 | 17.5 |

*Notes:* As for Table 6.3.

In the specialist, scale-intensive and traditional sectors, joint examination of Tables 6.4 and 6.5 confirms the conclusions reached earlier. In both specialist and scale-intensive sectors, probably because of the high initial technological competence of Italian firms, the foreign presence seems to stimulate growth of productivity in local firms. For these sectors, the substantial stability of the coefficients estimated for the *FOR* variables in all the regressions performed (see Tables 6.3–6.5) can apparently be explained by the fact that, in the majority of cases, the production frontier of the sector coincides with that of domestic firms. The results obtained therefore suggest that although the foreign presence might have not contributed to the transfer of foreign technologies, the competitive pressure generated by FDI has nonetheless induced local firms to make efforts to increase the productivity of the factors, and this gives rise to a greater aggregation of the techniques in use around the domestic production frontier. Also worth noting is the fact that the absolute value of the coefficient of the *FOR* variable is, in all the regressions, higher in the specialist sectors — where the competitive advantage of local firms over foreign ones was highlighted by the analysis conducted in the preceding sections. This confirms that the degree of initial technological competence of domestic industry is a significant determinant of the productive externalities associated with FDI.

## 6.5. CONCLUSIONS

The analysis proposed in the preceding sections has concentrated on two main aspects: the differing features of the domestic and foreign firms operating in Italy, and the supposed externalities on the performance of domestic firms generated by the presence of foreign firms.

As regards the former aspect, Sections 6.2 and 6.3 have shown that differences recorded in terms of labour productivity, of openness to exchanges with the rest of the world, and of productive internationalisation, reflect the well-known strengths and weaknesses of Italian industry. In the science-based sectors the weakness of Italian firms is obvious, especially if joint account is taken of the weight assumed by inward FDI in these sectors and of the gap between Italian and foreign firms in terms of the productivity of the factors. Added to the weakness of Italian industry is the fact that the majority of the more competitive firms in these sectors are foreign-owned. Moreover, the analysis conducted in Section 6.4 has shown that in these industrial sectors the foreign presence apparently does not induce the transfer of advanced technologies from foreign to local firms, nor does it encourage the aggregation of local firms around the domestic production frontier.

The specialist and traditional sectors, by contrast, confirm themselves as the spearhead of the national productive system. Added to the competitive advantage enjoyed by Italian industry in these sectors is the difficulty encountered by foreign MNEs in penetrating traditional ones. In the specialist sectors — characterised by a relatively intense foreign presence and by the high technological competence of Italian firms — the competition raised by the affiliates of foreign MNEs has seemingly prompted Italian firms to make greater efforts to increase their competitiveness. In traditional sectors, the modest amount of foreign presence in national industry is apparently responsible for the absence of causal relations between FDI and the performance of Italian firms.

The scale-intensive sectors are situated midway between these two extreme situations. On the one hand, the relative performances of Italian and foreign firms highlight the alternating strengths and weaknesses of the two groups of firms. On the other, added to the albeit weak signals of technological exchange between Italian and foreign firms is the apparently positive effect of the foreign presence on the ability of Italian firms to move closer to the domestic productive frontier.

As I have frequently mentioned, analysis of the effects of the foreign presence internally to the various industrial sectors or macro-sectors does not give an exhaustive account of the impact of the passive internationalisation of the Italian economy on the country's productive and innovative system. The specific features of Italian industry — in particular the complex interactions between small and medium-sized firms in the traditional and scale-intensive sectors on the one hand, and the producers of capital goods on the other — suggest that many of the effects of FDI may depend on its impact at the inter-industrial level, influencing the pattern of technological inter-relations among productive sectors. In this connection, a feature which prompts optimism concerning the development of Italian industry's competitive advantages consequent on FDI is the positive relation between foreign presence and the technical efficiency of domestic firms in specialist sectors. Given the characteristics of the Italian productive system as described above, this positive relation may boost the technological development of other industrial branches — the traditional sectors for example — apparently not influenced by the passive internationalisation of Italian industry.

## APPENDIX

### *Notes on the Construction of the Variables*

The number of employees in firms with foreign shareholding in each productive sector has been taken from the *Ricerche e Progetti* Reprint data bank, taking account of both majority and minority shareholdings. In order to construct the indices of penetration (the *FOR* variable), this variable was set in ratio to the total number of the employees of firms operating in Italy in each productive sector. These figures were taken from the ISTAT documentation on the number of workers in firms with more than 20 employees.

Since figures on capital at the level of the individual firm were not available, used as a proxy for this variable when constructing the *DEVKL* variable were the balance-sheet figures on plant and machinery contained in the *Mediocredito Centrale* data bank.

All the other data used for the econometric analysis can be obtained directly from this latter data bank.

Table A.6.1   Correspondences Between Sectors *à la* Pavitt and the ISTAT
Classification

| Sectors | ATECO81 |
| --- | --- |
| Chemicals derivatives | 255-256 |
| Pharmaceuticals | 257 |
| Office machinery and information technology | 330 |
| Electronics and telecommunications | 344-345 |
| Aircraft | 364 |
| Plant and machinery | 32 |
| Electromechanical | 342-348 |
| Precision machinery | 37 |
| Refined petroleum products | 140 |
| Primary metal products | 22 |
| Non-metallic minerals | 24 (esc.247) |
| Glass | 247 |
| Base chemicals | 251 |
| Consumer chemicals products | 258-259 |
| Artificial and synthetic fibres | 260 |
| Metal products | 31 |
| Electrical cables | 341 |
| Electrical components and products | 343-347 |
| Domestic appliances | 346 |
| Motor vehicles and bodywork | 351-352 |
| Components for motor vehicles | 353 |
| Other transport equipment | 36 (esc.364) |
| Derived foodstuffs | 413-419-421-423 |
| Beverages | 424-425-427-428 |
| Paper | 471-472 |
| Tyres and rubber products | 481-482 |
| Plastic products | 483 |
| Basic foodstuffs | 41(esc.413,419)-420-422 |
| Textiles | 43 |
| Clothing and leather goods | 44-45 |
| Timber and furniture | 46 |
| Printing and publishing | 473-474 |
| Other manufacturing industries | 49 |

Table A.6.2   Sales, Value Added, Exports and Employees in Italian and Foreign Firms: A Summary

| | Italian firms | | | | | Foreign firms | | | | |
|---|---|---|---|---|---|---|---|---|---|---|
| | Sales (millions of lire) | Value added (millions of lire) | Employee | Export/ Sales | Firms | Sales (millions of lire) | Value added (millions of lire) | Employee | Export/ Sales | Firms |
| Chemicals derivatives | 3777358 | 802342 | 14317 | 0.20 | 44 | 2485985 | 654714 | 7361 | 0.18 | 18 |
| Pharmaceuticals | 4507998 | 1658477 | 13360 | 0.06 | 30 | 7481964 | 2557489 | 21065 | 0.17 | 27 |
| Office machinery and information technology | 3981293 | 760410 | 17654 | 0.23 | 19 | 9150130 | 3288559 | 16173 | 0.38 | 5 |
| Electronics and telecommunications | 8746481 | 3316515 | 45635 | 0.10 | 80 | 8823714 | 3115855 | 37366 | 0.20 | 22 |
| Aircraft | 6370607 | 2585436 | 31678 | 0.16 | 13 | n.a. | n.a. | n.a. | n.a. | n.a. |
| **Science-based sectors** | **27383737** | **9123180** | **122644** | **0.14** | **186** | **27941793** | **9616617** | **81965** | **0.25** | **72** |
| Plant and machinery | 21333215 | 6792692 | 93437 | 0.47 | 473 | 7266566 | 1873684 | 27425 | 0.31 | 62 |
| Electromechanical | 6831764 | 2650554 | 35181 | 0.23 | 110 | 1031044 | 432342 | 5769 | 0.19 | 10 |
| Precision machinery | 2006681 | 796832 | 11644 | 0.36 | 46 | 1176529 | 345590 | 4138 | 0.12 | 9 |
| **Specialist sectors** | **30171660** | **10240078** | **140262** | **0.41** | **629** | **9474139** | **2651616** | **37332** | **0.27** | **81** |
| Refined petroleum products | 18236234 | 1967154 | 10686 | 0.08 | 14 | 10326097 | 515769 | 2418 | 0.12 | 5 |
| Primary metal products | 17549459 | 4395745 | 68633 | 0.21 | 117 | 2187837 | 513284 | 7741 | 0.38 | 13 |
| Non-metallic minerals | 9324412 | 3480178 | 41504 | 0.18 | 190 | 841654 | 354414 | 4026 | 0.22 | 9 |
| Glass | 1961208 | 825296 | 11152 | 0.11 | 38 | 633333 | 233646 | 2736 | 0.21 | 4 |
| Base chemicals | 10662561 | 2245733 | 25696 | 0.26 | 59 | 3258782 | 765878 | 8234 | 0.31 | 18 |
| Consumer chemicals products | 5018276 | 1132480 | 14644 | 0.29 | 19 | 2142242 | 607089 | 3902 | 0.07 | 8 |
| Artificial and synthetic fibres | 1921491 | 635604 | 7655 | 0.23 | 9 | n.a. | n.a. | n.a. | n.a. | n.a. |
| Metal products | 16429975 | 5488537 | 81440 | 0.24 | 495 | 35071516 | 2129946 | 24561 | 0.03 | 48 |
| Electrical cables | 2107808 | 563145 | 10449 | 0.15 | 15 | 634121 | 217563 | 2465 | 0.17 | 2 |

| | | | | | | | | | |
|---|---|---|---|---|---|---|---|---|---|
| Electrical components and products | 4735996 | 1561142 | 23357 | 0.22 | 79 | 2590304 | 1028738 | 13761 | 0.41 | 12 |
| Domestic appliances | 5618090 | 1609511 | 23590 | 0.29 | 42 | 4359588 | 1428686 | 19184 | 0.63 | 8 |
| Motor vehicles and bodywork | 29872959 | 6437836 | 155201 | 0.04 | 26 | 9101084 | 1681397 | 28188 | 0.54 | 4 |
| Components for motor vehicles | 2165808 | 826429 | 11559 | 0.22 | 30 | 1043177 | 342447 | 6173 | 0.22 | 9 |
| Other transport equipment | 4972604 | 1505060 | 31620 | 0.20 | 26 | 487274 | 196823 | 3519 | 0.35 | 6 |
| Derived foodstuffs | 12942998 | 2885106 | 26492 | 0.04 | 82 | 5124520 | 1321619 | 15490 | 0.13 | 5 |
| Beverages | 2328632 | 673789 | 6605 | 0.04 | 28 | 1480529 | 345001 | 3538 | 0.09 | 8 |
| Paper | 7052415 | 2461495 | 31567 | 0.19 | 105 | 1016534 | 307486 | 3356 | 0.29 | 13 |
| Tyres and rubber products | 4116922 | 1608451 | 22450 | 0.18 | 38 | 1931633 | 853378 | 11143 | 0.43 | 6 |
| Plastic products | 3044500 | 915686 | 12690 | 0.25 | 153 | 745410 | 270559 | 4309 | 0.43 | 15 |
| **Scale intensive sectors** | **160062348** | **41218377** | **616990** | **0.15** | **1565** | **82975635** | **13113723** | **164744** | **0.20** | **193** |
| Basic foodstuffs | 11044648 | 2261445 | 22107 | 0.07 | 102 | 1810941 | 218402 | 2389 | 0.09 | 9 |
| Textiles | 12556043 | 4072946 | 67632 | 0.26 | 339 | 823215 | 214559 | 4469 | 0.51 | 14 |
| Clothing and leather goods | 12450190 | 3155722 | 63823 | 0.32 | 402 | 627498 | 146212 | 2226 | 0.43 | 8 |
| Timber and furniture | 3913986 | 1018694 | 17519 | 0.29 | 166 | 64596 | 22389 | 337 | 0.56 | 3 |
| Printing and publishing | 8039012 | 3050146 | 32130 | 0.10 | 198 | 161500 | 41190 | 419 | 0.03 | 7 |
| Other manufacturing industries | 1969166 | 356934 | 6527 | 0.30 | 64 | 185140 | 51740 | 364 | 0.21 | 4 |
| **Traditional sectors** | **49973045** | **13915887** | **209738** | **0.21** | **1271** | **3672890** | **694492** | **10204** | **0.25** | **45** |
| **Total** | **267590790** | **74497522** | **1089634** | **0.19** | **3651** | **124064457** | **26076448** | **294245** | **0.21** | **391** |

*Note:* n.a. = not available.
*Source:* My calculations on data from *Mediocredito Centrale*.

# 7. Conclusions: Towards a Systemic Approach to Internationalisation Processes

## 7.1. INTRODUCTION

In the preceding chapters, I have sought to give an account of the interrelations among technological conditions, selective processes, passive processes of the internationalisation of economic systems, and industrial policies, while also assessing their impact on the development of the competitive advantages of industry in countries receiving direct investment from foreign MNEs.

From an analytical point of view, I have repeatedly pointed out that these effects come about, not according to the value assumed by one particular variable at a given point in time, but in relation to the combined values of the major economic magnitudes and to their evolution over time. For example, I have argued that that the same levels of the variables representing the foreign presence and the technological laggardliness of domestic firms with respect to foreign competitors may generate virtuous or vicious circles of development according to the pace with which foreign investments enter the country. Likewise I have argued that decisions by foreign MNEs concerning the type and quantity of technology to import into the country is a variable endogenous to the system, since it depends on the competitive pressure exerted by local firms or, in other words, on the degree of technological development that they have achieved.

Corresponding to every point in time, therefore, there is a systemic interdependence among the various variables and actors examined analytically in Chapter 3. The reactive capacity of domestic firms influences the importing of technology by the subsidiaries of foreign MNEs. The dynamics of the market shares of each firm are regulated by the evolution of its competitive advantages with respect to the other firms present in the market. In their turn, market shares together with the level of technological development determine profits and, consequently, the amount of resources available for R&D activity and, hence, the technological performance of each firm. The competitive regime and government policy then exert a pervasive influence on the dynamics of the variables just described by regulating the cause-and-effect relationship among them.

The empirical analysis conducted in Chapters 5 and 6 established the existence of important relations between the level of technological development of local industry and its ability to react to the presence of foreign firms on the national territory. Moreover, at least as regards British manufacturing industry, there is evidence of a significant link between the level reached by the foreign presence and the reactive capacity of domestic firms: a wide technological gap fully manifests its deleterious effect on the technological development of the indigenous industrial system when it is accompanied by the deep penetration of foreign MNEs into the national productive system. In the light of the analysis conducted in Chapter 3, this is because the displacement effect on local industry is in this case at its maximum, greatly reducing profits and, therefore, spending on R&D in domestic firms.

A great deal of work still remains to be done in empirical verification of these hypotheses. The statistical and econometric calculations presented in this book have been strongly conditioned by the scarcity and frequent unavailability of data. Moreover, as I have repeatedly stressed, the changing forms assumed by the processes of productive internationalisation require constant revision of the hypotheses formulated in relation to a given period or country, so that they may be adapted to different socioeconomic and cultural contexts.

For these reasons, providing a detailed list of the things to be done by empirical analysis is probably pointless. I have therefore preferred to devote the final pages of this book to a number of more general aspects of productive internationalisation which, in my view, warrant more detailed analysis. These aspects centre on the linkages among the various processes of the internationalisation of national productive and innovative systems, and on the problems raised by these processes for the study of the evolution of economic systems.

In this as in most other analyses of international production, attention has focused on only one of the many facets of the problem: namely, the consequences for the development of competitive advantages by indigenous firms of the passive internationalisation of industrial systems, where the latter expression is understood to include both the set of relations among the components of the national economy engaged in the production of goods (the productive system) and the relations among those of its components engaged in the production of scientific and technological innovations (the innovative system).[1]

The problems encountered by economic science in its endeavour to explain the processes of productive internationalisation by relying on traditional theory — dominated, on the one hand, by the neoclassical explanation of international trade and, on the other, by developments of transaction cost theory and the dichotomous choice between the granting of licences to independent firms and FDI — have for long overshadowed the interrelations among the various processes of internationalisation. However, recent research seems to have taken considerable steps in this direction, even though it starts from very different premises. This therefore seems an appropriate moment to review those various approaches that take some account of the unitary nature of the internationalisation of industrial systems and to conduct brief discussion of possible future developments of economic analysis in this area.

## 7.2. THE INTERNATIONALISATION OF PRODUCTIVE AND INNOVATIVE SYSTEMS: SOME REMARKS

As already mentioned, the essence of the problem consists in the interrelations among the various forms assumed by the internationalisation of national productive and innovative systems. Thus required, therefore, is analysis of how international

---

[1] Obviously, the more innovative processes arise from non-formalised sources, i.e. the less innovations are produced by *ad hoc* institutions (R&D laboratories, universities, public research centres, etc.), the more the productive and innovative systems will tend to coincide.

trade, direct investments abroad by resident firms, domestic investments by non-resident firms, international agreements for cooperation among firms, and technological transactions, interact with each other in the growth of the modern industrialised economies.

From a general point of view, the various forms assumed by the internationalisation of economic systems are merely parts of a broader system comprising the innovative and productive systems of the countries brought into contact by the internationalisation process. The essential feature of these relations is the fact that the linking mechanism among them is not a passive element or subsystem; instead, this mechanism is itself an important factor in shaping the evolution of national systems and it, too, is subject to evolutionary dynamics of development which react to forces internal to internationalisation processes themselves and to changes in the underlying productive and innovative systems. By mobilising a country's technical and scientific knowledge, by encouraging the exchange of information, goods and production factors, by expanding the sphere of action of competitive processes among firms, the internationalisation of economic systems is both one of the most powerful engines of their development and one of the major causes of their decline.

Providing an explanation of these dynamics is generally well beyond the scope of current studies on international economics or international business. Indeed, the majority of such studies concentrate on individual aspects of the internationalisation of economic systems, or else they fail to trace the consequences generated by the growing international integration consequent on the complex linkages that establish themselves among different economic systems. Nevertheless, the vast literature on the internationalisation of economic systems comprises a number of works which more closely approach the root of the problem.

Firstly, there are several recent studies which, although they move in highly diverse directions, all explicitly seek to highlight the interrelations among the various aspects of the internationalisation process and, in some cases, between these and the development of national productive and innovative systems. An example is provided by the ongoing line of research into the common determinants of international trade and of the FDI entering or leaving a country (Narula, 1995; Narula and Wakelin, 1995). The idea — developed from a neo-Schumpeterian standpoint — is that the competitiveness of a country is determined by the degree of development of its innovative system. The latter influences the country's trade performance and the internationalisation of its firms, and its attractiveness to firms in other countries wishing to locate abroad. The results of the econometric analyses set out in Narula and Wakelin's paper confirm *inter alia* the existence of significant relations between "country characteristics", on the one hand, and exports and foreign investments entering or leaving the country on the other. A second example of new lines of inquiry currently under development is the article by Mowery and Oxley (1995) on the role of innovative systems in the international transfer of technology to the economies of South-East Asia. In the light of the complementary nature of the various available forms of access to the technological resources of the more developed countries, Mowery and Oxley construct a set of statistics on the various internationalisation processes undertaken by these economies (foreign investments, joint ventures, strategic alliances, technological balance of payments, the importing of machinery, and engineering contracts) and outline the role played by government policies in delaying or accelerating the absorption of the advanced countries' technologies, and in helping or hindering the development of domestic industry.

A second strand of research concerns itself with national innovative systems (Dosi *et al.*, 1988; Lundvall, 1992; Nelson, 1993). This is evidently a line of inquiry that both logically and chronologically precedes the above studies, which expressly take the existence of these systems to be the basis for subsequent analysis. The difference is mainly one of emphasis, inasmuch as the existence and effectiveness of national boundaries is the analytical premise for study of the characteristics of each system-country. The principal focus is therefore on national systems isolated from the international context for the sake of analytical convenience. This strand of research nevertheless contains important studies which seek to direct attention to the implications for national innovative systems of the internationalisation processes guided by international trade and by the actions of the MNEs (see, for example, Chesnais, 1988 and 1992).

A third theoretical approach taking at least partial account of the interrelations among the internationalisation processes of industrial systems, and of the impact of these processes on the development of the economies concerned, comprises studies which analyse competition among rival industrial systems. In this case, a distinction must be drawn between at least two sub-strands of inquiry. The first has its most outstanding representative in Michael Porter, and takes the 'diamond of competitive advantages' as its main analytical scheme. The second substrand has been most thoroughly developed in the work of John Cantwell, which examines the cause and effect processes generated by technological competition between multinational and uninational firms from different countries.

In its original formulation (Porter, 1990), Porter's approach starts from an analytical premise very different from the one advanced here. He believes that the building of a country's competitive advantages takes place at the national rather than international level. Although Porter acknowledges the possible influence of the internationalisation of production on the building of national competitive advantages, he apparently believes them to be of secondary importance compared with exploitation of the opportunities offered by the domestic environment, and he repeatedly expresses serious concern over the possible negative effects on national industry of a massive inflow of foreign firms.

As Dunning (1994b) has stressed, the principal weakness in Porter's analysis of the internationalisation of national productive systems is its failure to include a further vertex representing the activity of MNEs in the diamond of competitive advantages. If Porter had done so, his analysis of various countries would probably be more complete, because it would highlight their peculiarities in terms of the extent to which national economies rely on foreign inputs to their industrial systems. Dunning performs this operation, but his analytical effort is somewhat compromised by the fact that, instead of regarding the activities of MNEs as an further element interacting with the other vertexes of the diamond, he introduces international production as a factor endogenous to the system.

Much further ahead in the study of the consequences of industrial internationalisation on the development of national innovative and productive systems is the theoretical approach suggested by John Cantwell. This pivots, on the one hand, on technological competition among firms or groups of firms from different countries and, on the other, on the processes of technological and capitalist accumulation generated by the internationalisation of economic systems in different productive areas (Cantwell, 1989). From this theoretical perspective, which has been discussed on various occasions in this book, growing international movements of goods and production factors give rise in the countries concerned to the genesis or acceleration of cumulative processes of growth or decline of the national industries in relation to the ability of domestic firms to exploit the opportunities presented by the greater international mobility of goods or production factors or, conversely, to their inability to mobilise the resources necessary to combat competition by foreign firms.

The most interesting aspect of Cantwell's approach, as far as my present discussion is concerned, is that it enables specification of the different types of interaction among national productive and innovative systems generated by processes of industrial internationalisation (Cantwell, 1995a). An example arises when internationalisation leads to an encounter among highly developed industrial systems in the same product area. In this case, in fact, it becomes possible for all the countries involved to benefit from the stimuli created by stronger technological competition among firms from different countries for the control of world markets. The desire of firms to secure the competitive advantages of their rivals gives rise to reciprocal invasions of their areas of origin: they transplant their production systems, or they establish R&D centres, or they develop international cooperation agreements. This gives rise to a linkage among industrial systems excelling in the development of particular technologies which increases the cohesion among them and provides the basis for further processes of technological and capitalist accumulation. The diametrically opposite case arises when internationalisation processes displace the industry of the country receiving the commercial flows or the FDI. In this case, in fact, the encounter between the innovative and productive systems of different countries severely penalises the one subject to the passive internationalisation of its industrial system. The competing country's firms appropriate a proportion of the latter's national productive and innovative resources without this becoming a stimulus to the growth of its national industry.

## 7.3. INDICATIONS FOR FURTHER INQUIRY INTO INTERNATIONALISATION PROCESSES

The various strands of research briefly outlined in the previous chapter shed considerable light on the interrelations among the various components of the internationalisation processes of national productive and innovative systems, and between these processes and the development of the systems themselves. Nonetheless, I believe that further analysis is required in the areas that, in conclusion to this work, I now briefly describe.

First, the theoretical approach adopted in discussion of national innovative systems could be expanded by explicitly acknowledging the existence of relations or points of intersection among national systems engendered by the processes of industrial internationalisation. By way of example, contemporary economic discussion is often predicated on the existence of a triadic world economy consisting of the industrial systems of Western Europe, Japan and the United States. It thus recognises the existence of close interrelations among industrial systems which go beyond national borders, but it rarely passes from this recognition to analysis of the types of interaction that occur between the productive and the technological development of the European countries.

This, of course, is not to gainsay the unitary nature of national systems or to deny that the governments have room for manoeuvre in influencing the processes at the basis of national economic development. On the contrary, it is precisely the opportunity afforded to national systems to interact, in different ways and to different extents, with other systems that enhances the possibilities for manoeuvre of individual system-countries. The opportunities now available to the modern national industrial systems to utilise numerous channels of interconnection with the most developed economies is one of the distinctive features of the process whereby they build their competitive advantages. For example, the ability of the governments and entrepreneurial systems of certain South-East Asian countries to reap the benefits of the decentralisation of Japanese industry in the last few decades has been the decisive factor in the spectacular growth of those economies, and not, or at least not solely, their ability to mobilise the 'national attributes' of the system-country. In part by replicating the postwar experience of the Japanese economy, the strategy for success has been the efficient coordination of the different ways to acquire technologies and production factors from abroad, of macro-economic policies designed to ensure stability and to encourage major investment in human capital, of industrial policies aimed at increasing competitive stimuli for national firms on both the domestic and international markets (Mowery and Oxley, 1995).

It is precisely the experience of these countries that provides a valid example of the possible interconnections between national innovative and productive systems. In recent years, in fact, they seem not only to have reached levels of development comparable with those of the most industrialised countries; they have also inserted themselves into an international macrosystem which still today enables them to benefit from and to interact with the Japanese economy's further phases of development. This has occurred while these countries have endeavoured — with the strong growth of the internationalisation of their firms — to intersect with the lines of technological and industrial develop-ment of the Western economies.

Though it is to some extent subordinate to the one just discussed, there exists a further possibility for theoretical devel-opment, in the area of forms of interaction between national innovative and productive systems. This strand of inquiry comes very close to the analysis presented in this book, with its discussion of the consequences of direct investments by foreign MNEs on the industrial systems of the recipient countries, and its emphasis that the overall effect can be divided into two distinct components: positive externalities or spillovers, and the displacement effect on domestic industry.

One way to extend the results obtained in this and similar works would be to construct a typology corresponding to the encounter between different innovative and productive systems. Purely by way of illustration, three different forms of encounter can be isolated at the level of the individual industry or country.

Type 1 is complementarity between national innovative and productive systems. In this case the internationalisation of individual national economies enables the merger of scientific and technological knowledge which, although of differing ori-gin, is closely complementary. This process gives rise to a third innovative and productive system of international scope which produces positive externalities for all the countries involved.

Displacement effects are reduced to the minimum and they correspond at most to the reallocation of resources from industrial sectors in decline to those benefiting from the internationalisation of the economy. This type broadly comprises the South-East Asian economies discussed above.

The second type involves a relation of substitutability between competing innovative and productive systems. The internationalisation of country $A$'s firms into country $B$ leads to the substitution of local producers by foreign firms. There is maximum displacement of domestic firms and minimal technological spillovers for country $B$. Belonging to this type are, for example, the British industries characterised by rapid technological and scientific decline consequent on the massive FDI discussed in previous chapters.

Type 3 comprises completely (or almost) internationalised innovative and productive systems. Little has been said about these systems in previous chapters, since they are largely identifiable with the industrial systems of small-sized countries. In many of these cases, indeed, it is inappropriate to talk of national innovative and productive systems, so great is the role played by the international component in developing the competitive advantages of resident firms. These, in fact, are industrial systems which have for long made a virtue out of necessity by compensating for the small size of their domestic markets through the massive internationalisation of their productive systems. Belonging to this category are countries like Holland and Denmark which, for centuries, have exploited the opportunities offered by conducting their economic activities on a world scale.

The third and last area of inquiry is apparently unrelated to the first two but in reality closely connected to them. I refer to possible development of the theory of the firm in the light of internationalisation processes. The connection with the analytical developments discussed above becomes clear when one considers that (i) firms constitute the basic units of innovative and productive systems, and (ii) that they themselves are innovative and productive systems in miniature.

For a long time the theory of the firm has rested on two fundamental working hypotheses regarding processes of internationalisation. First, the choice among the different forms of internationalisation is a dichotomous choice between foreign investments and the granting of licences to independent firms;

or, more recently, it has become a trichotomous one by incorporating into the analytical scheme the growing number of
strategic alliances and joint ventures among firms from different countries. Second, internationalisation is a sequential process in which commercial flows towards a given country can be
replaced, in a subsequent phase, by FDI.

Both hypotheses will probably have to be revised in the light
of recent developments in the internationalisation of production, since they correspond to a passive, rather than active,
conception of entrepreneurial activity.

In fact, according to this theoretical framework, *given* a
certain set of environmental conditions mainly to do with the
*efficiency* of the markets internal and external to the organisation, a firm decides what proportion of its technical, productive
and commercial functions to perform internally or externally to
it, or whether to adopt mixed forms. From a different standpoint, *given* a certain structure of exports by a particular firm,
the political, social and economic conditions of outlet markets,
and the knowledge of these markets acquired from the firm's
past activity, the decision is taken whether to replace commercial flows with more evolved forms of internationalisation.

However, it is becoming increasingly evident that the processes of production internationalisation far exceed the forecasts of the mainstream theories. While the firms of the most
industrialised countries constantly invent new ways to involve
themselves in the economies of other countries while theoretical
analysis struggles to keep up, they are the increasingly active
agents of a process of development which views the various
forms of internationalisation as complementary rather than
alternative. A glance at the international ramifications of the
largest multinationals suffices to show that, in the majority of
cases, a firm in country $x$ involves itself in country $y$'s economic
system by means of a mix of activities comprising not only
commercial flows but FDI and joint ventures with resident
firms as well.

That there exist various directions of research able to close
the gap between theory and reality is certain. In all cases,
however, it is necessary to pass from a passive conception of the
firm to one that views the firm as the engine of internationalisation processes, and entrepreneurial activity as the driving
force of change. This is a conception that relates closely to the
theories of the classical economists and to the Schumpeterian

notion of creative destruction, while distancing itself from the neoclassical view of the firm as a maximising agent operating under close environmental constraints. Here I shall restrict my discussion to the two recent theoretical developments that strike me as most promising.

The first is based on the so-called 'extended version' of the eclectic approach to international production (Dunning, 1994b). According to this new version of what is now a classical approach, changes in the level and composition of the foreign activities of each MNE depend on two sets of interrelated and not easily isolable variables: the firm's response to changes in the structure of the OLI occurring independently of the firm's behaviour (strategy-led changes), and changes introduced by the firm itself in order to alter its own structure (strategy-initiating changes). The distinctive feature of the evolution of the processes of internationalisation is therefore *"the continuous interaction between changes in exogenous and (non strategic) endogenous variables and the strategic actions and reactions of firms."*[2]

The second development originates from research carried out by several authors with the purpose of developing an evolutionary theory of the processes of internationalisation of firms (Cantwell, 1992a, 1995a; Kogut and Zander, 1992, 1993; Zander and Kogut, 1995).[3] These analytical developments start from the conception of internationalisation processes employed by the transaction cost approach, and they proclaim that "the image of a 'decision' to internalise an activity is an artificial characterisation."[4] Rather, it is the 'combinative capability' of the firm — i.e. its ability constantly to re-elaborate its competitive advantages according to the stimuli and knowledge deriving from the external environment (Kogut and Zander, 1992) — that constitutes the core of its competitive advantages. In other words, firms are distinguished one from the other less by their possession of a stock of tangible or intangible activities, or by a set of market or hierarchical relations woven around an entrepreneurial nucleus, as in transaction costs theory, than by

---

[2] Dunning (1994b, p. 73).
[3] See also the vigorous debate provoked by Kogut and Zander's articles in the *Journal of International Business Literature*: Love (1995), McFetridge (1995), Kogut and Zander (1995).
[4] Kogut and Zander (1995), p. 425.

their ability constantly to change the content of these activities in order to maintain or improve their competitiveness. The firm is thus viewed as not only able to choose the best alternative among those available but also continually to create new alternatives on which depend the technological flows and interconnections among different innovative and productive systems that come about as a consequence of the firm's internationalisation.

# References

Aitken, B. and Harrison, A. (1991), Are there positive spillovers from foreign direct investment? Evidence from a panel data for Venezuela, World Bank, mimeo.

Balasubramanyam, V.N., Salisu, M. and Sapsford, D. (1996), Foreign direct investment and growth in EP and IP countries, *Economic Journal*, **106**, 92–105.

Balloni, V. (1995), Squilibri strutturali e nuovi assetti dell'industria italiana, paper presented at the conference "Differenziali di sviluppo e disoccupazione nella economia italiana", University of Rome "La Sapienza".

Baran, P.A. and Sweezy, P.M. (1966), *Monopoly Capital*, Monthly Review Press, New York.

Baumol, W.J., Blackman, B. and Wolff, E.N. (1989), *Productivity and American Leadership*, MIT Press, Cambridge (Mass.).

Behrman, J. and Wallender, H. (1976), *Transfer of Manufacturing Technology between Multinational Enterprises*, Ballinger, Cambridge (Mass.).

Bhagwati, J.N. (1978), *Anatomy and Consistency of Exchange Control Regimes*, Studies in International Economic Relations, Vol. I, n. 10, NBER, New York.

Bhagwati, J.N. (1985), *Investing Abroad*, Esmée Fairbain Lecture, Lancaster University.

Blomstrom, M. (1986), Foreign investment and productive efficiency: the case of Mexico, *Journal of Industrial Economics*, **15**, 97–110.

Blomstrom, M. (1989), *Foreign Investment and Spillovers: A Study of Technology Transfer to Mexico*, Routledge, London.

Blomstrom, M. (1991), Host country benefits of foreign investment, in D. McFetridge (Ed.), *Foreign Investment Technology and Economic Growth*, University of Calgary Press, Calgary.

Blomstrom, M. and Kokko, A. (1993), Policies to encourage inflows of technology through foreign multinationals, NBER Working Paper No. 4289.

Blomstrom, M., Kokko, A. and Zejan, M. (1992), Host country competition and technology transfer by multinationals, NBER Working Paper No. 4131.

Blomstrom, M. and Persson, H. (1983), Foreign direct investment and spillover efficiency in an underdeveloped economy: evidence from the Mexican manufacturing industry, *World Development*, **11**, 493–501.

Blomstrom, M. and Wolff, E.N. (1989), Multinational corporations and productivity convergence in Mexico, NBER Working Paper No. 3141, reprinted in W. Baumol, R.R. Nelson and E. Wolff (Eds.) (1994) *International Convergence of Productivity: Cross-National Studies and Historical Perspectives*, Oxford University Press, Oxford.

Blomstrom, M. and Wolff, E.N. (1993), Growth in a dual economy, New York University, C.V. Starr Center for Applied Economics, Economic Research Report No. 93-40.

Brash, D.T. (1966), *American Investment in Australian Industry*, Harvard University Press, Cambridge (Mass.).

Brech, M. and Sharp, M. (1984), *Inward Investment: Policy Options for the United Kingdom*, Chatam House Papers n. 21, Routledge & Kegan Paul, London.

Buckley, P.J. (1985), The economic analysis of the multinational enterprise: Reading versus Japan?, *Hitotsubashi Journal of Economics*, **26**, 2.

Buckley, P.J. and Casson, M. (1976), *The Future of the Multinational Enterprise*, Macmillan, London.

Buckley, P.J. and Casson, M. (Eds.) (1992), *Multinational Enterprises in the World Economy: Essays in Honour of John Dunning*, Edward Elgar, Aldershot.

Cainarca, G. (1992), L'investimento diretto estero nell'industria italiana, in Cominotti R. and Mariotti S. (Eds.), *Italia Multinazionale 1992*, ETAS Libri, Milano.

Cantwell, J.A. (1987), The reorganisation of European industries after integration: selected evidences on the role of multinational enterprise activities, *Journal of Common Market Studies*, **26**, reprinted in J.H. Dunning and P. Robson (Eds.), *Multinational and the European Community*, Basil Blackwell, Oxford.

Cantwell, J.A. (1989), *Technological Innovation and Multinational Corporations*, Basil Blackwell, Oxford.

Cantwell, J.A. (1991), A survey of theories of international production, in C.N. Pitelis and R. Sugden (Eds.), *The Nature of Transnational Firm*, Routledge, London.

Cantwell, J.A. (1992a), Innovation and technological competitiveness, in P.J. Buckley and M. Casson (Eds.), *Multinational Enterprises in the World Economy: Essays in Honour of John Dunning*, Edward Elgar, Aldershot.

Cantwell, J.A. (1992b), The effects of integration on the structure of multinational corporation activity in the EC, in M.W. Klein and P.J.J. Welfens (Eds.), *Multinationals in the New Europe and Global Trade*, Springer-Verlag, Berlin.

Cantwell, J.A. (1993), Technological competence and evolving patterns of international production, in H. Cox, J. Clegg and G. Ietto-Giles (Eds.), *The Growth of Global Business*, Routledge, London.

Cantwell, J.A. (1995a), Multinational corporations and innovatory activities: towards a new, evolutionary approach, in J. Molero (Ed.), *Technological Innovation, Multinational Corporations and New International Competitiveness: The Case of Intermediate Countries*, Harwood Academic Publishers.

Cantwell, J.A. (1995b), The globalisation of technology: what remains of the product cycle model?, *Cambridge Journal of Economics*, **19**, 155–174.

Cantwell, J.A. and Dunning, J.H. (1991), MNEs technology and the competitiveness of European industry, *Aussenwirtschaft*, **46**, 45–65.

Cantwell, J.A. and Sanna Randaccio, F. (1992), Intra-industry direct investment in the European Community: oligopolistic rivalry and technological competition, in J.A. Cantwell (Ed.), *Multinational Investment in Modern Europe: Strategic Interaction in the Integrated Economy*, Edward Elgar, Aldershot.

Casson, M. (1991), Internalization theory and beyond, in P.J. Buckley (Ed.), *Recent Research on the Multinational Enterprise*, Edward Elgar, London.

Caves, R.E. (1974), Multinational firms, competition and productivity in host-country markets, *Economica*, **41**, 176–193.

Chen, E.K.Y. (1983), *Multinational Corporations, Technology and Employment*, Macmillan, London.

Chesnais, F. (1988), Multinational enterprises and the international diffusion of technology, in G. Dosi, C. Freeman, R. Nelson, G. Silverberg and L. Soete (Eds.), *Technical Change and Economic Theory*, Pinter Publishers, London.

Chesnais, F. (1992), National systems of innovation, foreign direct investment and the operations of multinational enterprises, in B.A. Lundvall (Ed.), *National Systems of Innovation*, Pinter Publishers, London.

Coase, R.H. (1937), The nature of the firm, *Economica*, **4**, November, 386–405.

Cohen, W.M. and Levinthal, D.A. (1989), Innovation and learning: the two faces of R&D, *Economic Journal*, **99**, 569–596.

Cominotti, R. and Mariotti, S. (Eds.) (1990), *Italia Multinazionale 1990*, Etas Libri, Milano.

Cominotti, R. and Mariotti, S. (Eds.) (1992), *Italia Multinazionale 1992*, Etas Libri, Milano.

Cominotti, R. and Mariotti, S. (Eds.) (1994), *Italia Multinazionale 1994*, Etas Libri, Milano.

Cowling, K. and Sugden, R. (1987), *Transnational Monopoly Capitalism*, Wheatsheaf Books, Brighton.

Das, S. (1987), Externalities and technology transfer through multinational corporations, *Journal of International Economics*, **90**, 1142–1165.

Dosi, G. and Fabiani, S. (1994), Convergence and divergence in the long-term growth of open economies, in G. Silverberg and L. Soete (Eds.), *The Economics of Growth and Technological Change*, Edward Elgar, Aldershot.

Dosi, G. and Freeman, C. (1992), The diversity of development patterns: on the process of catching-up, forging ahead and falling behind, paper presented at the *International Economic Association Meeting*, Varenna, Italy, 1–3 October.

Dosi, G., Freeman C., Nelson, R.R., Silverberg, G. and Soete, L. (Eds.) (1988), *Technical Change and Economic Theory*, Pinter Publishers, London.

Dunning, J.H. (1958), *American Investment in British Manufacturing Industry*, Allen and Unwin, London.

Dunning, J.H. (1981), *International Production and the Multinational Enterprises*, Allen and Unwin, London.

Dunning, J.H. (1982), Explaining the international direct investment position of countries: towards a dynamic or developmental approach, in J. Black and J.H. Dunning (Eds.), *International Capital Movements*, Macmillan, London.

Dunning, J.H. (1985) (Ed.), *Multinational Enterprises, Economic Structure and International Competitiveness*, IRM/Wiley Series on Multinational, John Wiley and Sons, Chichester.

Dunning, J.H. (1986), *Japanese Participation in the British Industry*, Croom Helm, London.

Dunning, J.H. (1988a), *Multinationals, Technology and Competitiveness*, Allen and Unwin, London.

Dunning, J.H. (1988b), *Explaining International Production*, Allen and Unwin, London.

Dunning, J.H. (1992), Multinational enterprises and the global innovatory capacity, in O. Granstand, L. Hakanson and S. Sjolander (Eds.), *Technology Management* and *International Business, Internationalisation of R&D and Technology*, John Wiley and Sons, Chichester.

Dunning, J.H. (1994a), Multinational enterprises and the globalisation of innovatory capacity, *Research Policy*, **23**, 67–88.

Dunning, J.H. (1994b), *The Globalisation of Business: The Challenge of the 1990s*, Routledge, London.

Findlay, R. (1978), Relative backwardness, direct foreign investment, and the transfer of technology: a simple dynamic model, *Quarterly Journal of Economics*, **92**, 1–16.

Forsyth, D. (1972), *US Investment in Scotland*, Praeger, New York.

Freeman, C. (Ed.) (1990), *The Economics of Innovations*, Edward Elgar, Aldershot.

Fujita, K. and Hill, R.C. (1995), Global toyotaism and local development, *Urban Affairs Review*, **1**, 7–22.

Gailbraith, J.K. (1971), *The New Industrial State*, Andre Deutsch, London.

Galton, F. (1889), *Natural Inheritance*, Macmillan, London.

Gerschenberg, I. (1987), The training and spread of managerial know-how. A comparative analysis of multinational and other firms in Kenya, *World Development*, **15**, 931–939.

Gerschenkron, A. (1962), *Economic Backwardness in Historical Perspective*, Harvard University Press, Cambridge (Mass.).

Globerman, S. (1979), Foreign direct investment and spillover efficiency benefits in Canadian manufacturing industries, *Canadian Journal of Economics*, **12**, 42–56.

Globerman, S. and Meredith, L. (1984), The foreign ownership-innovation nexus in Canada, *Columbia Journal of World Business*, **19**, 53–62.

Globerman, S., Ries, J.C. and Vertinsky, I. (1994), The economic performance of foreign affiliates in Canada, *Canadian Journal of Economics*, **27**, 143–156.

Graham, E.M. (1975), Oligopolistic Imitation and European Direct Investment, Ph.D. Dissertation, Harvard Graduate School of Business Administration.

Graham, E.M. (1978), Transatlantic investment by multinational firms: a rivalistic phenomenon?, *Journal of Post Keynesian Economics*, **1**, 82–99.

Graham, E.M. (1985), Intra-industry direct investment, market structure, firm rivalry and technological performance, in A. Erdilek (Ed.), *Multinationals as Mutual Invaders: Intra-industry Direct Foreign Investment*, Croom Helm, London.

Graham, E.M. and Krugman, P.R. (1989), *Foreign Direct Investment in the United States*, Institute for International Economics, Washington DC.

Haddad, M. and Harrison, A. (1993), Are there positive spillovers from direct foreign investment? Evidence from panel data for Morocco, *Journal of Economic Development*, **42**, 51–74.

Hart, P.E. (1976), The dynamics of earnings, 1960–1973, *Economic Journal*, **86**, 551–565.

Hart, P.E. and Prais, S.J. (1956), The analysis of business concentration: a statistical approach, *Journal of the Royal Statistical Society, series A*, **119**.

Hirschman, A.O. (1958), *The Strategy of Economic Development*, Yale University Press, New Haven.

Hughes, K. (1993), Foreign multinationals and economic competitiveness: the UK experience, in M. Humbert (Ed.), *The Impact of Globalisation on Europe's Firms and Industries*, Pinter Publishers, London.

Hymer, S. (1960), *The International Operations of National Firms: A Study of Direct Investment*, Ph.D. thesis, MIT (published by MIT Press in 1976).

Hymer, S. (1968), La grande firme multinationale, *Revue Economique*, **14**, 949–973. Translated in English in M.C. Casson (Ed.), *Multinational Corporations*, Edward Elgar, Cheltenam.

Hymer, S. (1970), The efficiency (contradictions) of multinational corporations, *American Economic Review*, **60**, May, 441–448.

JETRO (1995), *The 11th Survey of European Operations of Japanese Companies in the Manufacturing Sector*, JETRO, London.

Kamien, M. and Schwartz, N. (1982), *Market Structure and Innovation*, Cambridge University Press, Cambridge.

Katz, J.M. (1969), *Production Functions, Foreign Investment and Growth*, North Holland, Amsterdam.

Katz, J.M. (1987), *Technology Creation in Latin American Manufacturing Industries*, St. Martin's Press, New York.

Kindleberger, C.P. (1969), *American Business Abroad: Six Lectures on Direct Investment*, Yale University Press, New Haven.

Kogut, B. and Zander, U. (1992), Knowledge of the firm, combinative capabilities, and the replication of technology, *Organization Science*, **3**, 383–397.

Kogut, B. and Zander, U. (1993), Knowledge of the firm and the evolutionary theory of the multinational corporation, *Journal of International Business Studies*, **24**, 625–645.

Kogut, B. and Zander, U. (1995), Knowledge, market failure and the multinational enterprise: a reply, *Journal of International Business Studies*, **26**, 417–426.

Koizumi, T. and Kopeck, K.J. (1977), Economic growth, capital movements and the international transfer of technical knowledge, *Journal of International Economics*, **7**, 45–65.

Kojima, K. (1978), *Direct Foreign Investment: a Japanese Model of Multinational Business Operations*, Croom Helm, London.

Kojima, K. and Ozawa, T. (1985), Toward a theory of industrial restructuring and dynamic comparative advantages, *Hitotsubashi Journal of Economics*, **26**, 2.

Kokko, A. (1992), *Foreign Direct Investment, Host Country Characteristics and Spillovers*, Stockholm School of Economics, Stockholm.

Kristensen, T. (1974), *Development in Rich and Poor Countries*, Praeger, New York.

Lake, J.M. (1979), Technology creation and technology transfer by multinational firms, in R.G. Hawkins (Ed.), *Research in International Business and Finance: The Effects of Multinational Corporations*, Vol. 1, JAI Press, Greenwich, Connecticut.

Lall, S. (1978), Transnationals, domestic enterprises, and industrial structure in host LDCs: a survey, *Oxford Economic Papers*, **30**, 217–248.

Lall, S. (1980), Vertical inter-firm linkages in LDCs: an empirical study, *Oxford Bulletin of Economics and Statistics*, **42**, 203–226.

Lall, S. and Streeten, P. (1977), *Foreign Investment, Transnationals and Developing Countries*, Macmillan, London.

Lenin, V.I. (1939), *Imperialism: The Highest Stage of Capitalism* (page numbers refer to the English edition, International Publishers, New York, 1977).

Levy, D. and Dunning, J.H. (1993), International production and sourcing: trends and issues, *STI Review*, n. 13, 13–59.

Love, J.H. (1995), Knowledge, market failure and the multinational enterprise: a theoretical note, *Journal of International Business Studies*, **26**, 399–407.

Lundvall, B.A. (Ed.) (1992), *The National Systems of Innovation: Towards a Theory of Innovation and Interactive Learning*, Pinter Publishers, London.

Mansfield, E. (1961), Technical change and the rate of imitation, *Econometrica*, **29**, 741–766.

Mansfield, E. (1968), *Industrial Research and Technological Innovation*, Norton, New York.

Mansfield, E. and Romeo, A. (1980), Technology transfer to overseas subsidiaries by US-based firms, *Quarterly Journal of Economics*, **95**, 737–750.

Mariotti, S. (1988), Italian inward and outward direct investment: a comparison, in F. Onida and G. Viesti (Eds.), *The Italian Multinationals*, London, Croom Helm.

Mariotti, S. (1992), L'internazionalizzazione dell'industria italiana, in R. Cominotti and S. Mariotti (Eds.), *Italia Multinazionale 1992*, ETAS Libri, Milano.

Marx, K. (1859), *Grundisse: Introduction to the Critique of Political Economy* (page numbers refer to the English edition, Vintage, New York, 1973).

McAleese, D. and McDonald, D. (1978), Employment growth and development of linkages in foreign-owned and domestic manufacturing enterprises, *Oxford Bulletin of Economics and Statistics*, **40**.

McFetridge, D.G. (1995), Knowledge, market failure and the multinational enterprise: a comment, *Journal of International Business Studies*, **26**, 409–415.

McManus, J.C. (1972), The theory of the international firm, in G. Paquet (Ed.), *The Multinational Firm and the Nation State*, Collier-Macmillan, Toronto.

Mediocredito Centrale (1994), *Indagine sulle imprese manifatturiere. Quinto rapporto sull'industria italiana e sulla politica industriale*, Milano, Il Sole 24 Ore.

Molteni, C. (1994), Japanese joint ventures in Italy: a new second best strategy?, in N. Campbell and F. Burton (Eds.), *Japanese Multinationals: Strategies and Management in the Global Kaisha*, London, Routledge.

Moran, T.H. (1970), Multinational corporations and dependency: a dialogue for dependentistas and non-dependentistas, *International Organisation*, **32**, 79–100.

Mowery, D. and Oxley, J.E. (1995), Inward technology transfer and competitiveness: the role of national innovation systems, *Cambridge Journal of Economics*, **19**, 67–93.

Narula, R. (1996), *Multinational Investment and Economic Structure*, Routledge, London.

Narula, R. and Wakelin, K. (1995), Technological competitiveness, trade and foreign direct investment, in R. Schiattarella (Ed.), *New Challenges for European and International Business*, Vol. 2, Proceedings of the 21st Annual Conference of the European International Business Academy, Urbino, Italy, 10–12 December.

Nelson, R.R. (Ed.) (1993), *National Innovation Systems: A Comparative Analysis*, Oxford University Press, Oxford.

Newfarmer, R.S. (Ed.) (1985), *Profits, Progress and Poverty: Case Studies of International Industries in Latin America*, University of Notre Dame Press, Notre Dame, IN.

Oliver, N. and Wilkinson, B. (1988), *The Japanisation of British Industry*, Basil Blackwell, Oxford.

Patel, P. (1995), Localised production of technology for global markets, *Cambridge Journal of Economics*, **19**, 141–153.

Patel, P. and Pavitt, K. (1991) Large firms in the production of the world's technology: an important case of non-globalisation, *Journal of International Business Studies*, **22**, 1–21.

Pavitt, K. (1971), The multinational enterprise and the transfer of technology, in J.H. Dunning (Ed.), *The Multinational Enterprise*, Allen & Unwin, London.

Pavitt, K. (1984), Sectoral patterns of technological change: towards a taxonomy and a theory, *Research Policy*, **13**, 343–373.

Perez, T. (1997), Multinational enterprises and technological spillovers: An evolutionary model, *Journal of Evolutionary Economics*, n. 7, 169–192.

Piscitello, L. (1994), L'investimento diretto estero nell'industria italiana, in R. Cominotti and S. Mariotti (Eds.), *Italia Multinazionale 1994*, Etas Libri, Milano.

Porter, M. (1990), *The Competitive Advantages of Nations*, Free Press, New York.

Ramazzotti, P. (1995), Italy and Japanese multinationals, paper presented at the conference *Japan and the Peripheral Regions of Europe*, Belfast, 9–11 March.

Ray, G.F. (1990), International labour costs in manufacturing, 1960–1988, *National Institute Economic Review*, n. 132 (May), 67–70.

Robock, S.H. (1980), *The International Technology Transfer Process*, National Academy of Science, Washington DC.

Rostow, W.W. (1980), *Why the Poor Get Richer and the Rich Slow Down: Essays in the Marshallian Long Period*, Macmillan, London.

Safarian, A.E. (1966), *Foreign Ownership of Canadian Industry*, McGraw-Hill, Toronto.

Savary, J. (1984), *French Multinationals*, Pinter Publishers, London.

Schumpeter, J.A. (1928), The instability of capitalism, *Economic Journal*, 361–386.

Schumpeter, J.A. (1934), *The Theory of Economic Development: An Enquiry into Profits, Capital, Credit Interest and Business Cycle*, Oxford University Press, London.

Schumpeter, J.A. (1942), *Capitalism, Socialism and Democracy*, McGraw Hill, New York.

Silverberg, G., Dosi, G. and Orsenigo, L. (1988), Innovation, diversity and diffusion: A self-organisation model, *Economic Journal*, **98**, 1032–1054.

Stoneman, P. (1989), Overseas financing for industrial R&D in the UK, Paper delivered to the British Association, September.

Strange, R. (1993), *Japanese Manufacturing Investment in Europe. Its Impact on the UK Economy*, Routledge, London.

Teece, D.J. (1977), Technology transfer by multinational firms: the resource cost of transferring technological know-how, *The Economic Journal*, **87**, 242–262.

Teece, D.J., Pisano, G. and Shuen, A. (1990), Firm capabilities, resources, and the concept of strategy, mimeo, University of California, Berkeley.

Tilton, G.E. (1971), *The International Diffusion of Technology: The Case of Semiconductors*, Brookings Institutions, Washington.

UNCTC (1992), *World Investment Report*, United Nations Transnational Corporations and Management Division, New York.

US Department of Commerce (1992), *US Direct Investment Abroad, 1989 Benchmark Survey, Final Results*, US Department of Commerce, Washington DC.

Veblen T. (1915), *Imperial Germany and Industrial Revolution*, Macmillan, London.

Vernon, R. (1966), International investment and international trade in the product cycle, *Quarterly Journal of Economics*, **80**, 190–207.

Vernon, R. (1974), The location of economic activity, in J.H. Dunning (Ed.), *Economic Analysis and the Multinational Enterprises*, Allen and Unwin, London.

Vernon, R. (1979), The product cycle hypothesis in the new international environment, *Oxford Bulletin of Economics and Statistics*, **41**, 255–267.

Verspagen, B. (1993), *Uneven Growth Between Interdependent Economies*, Avebury, Aldershot.

Veugelers, R. and Vanden Houte, R. (1990), Domestic R&D in the presence of multinational enterprise, *International Journal of Industrial Organisation*, **8**, 1–15.

Wang, Y. and Blomstrom, M. (1992), Foreign investment and technology transfer: a simple model, *European Economic Review*, **36**, 137–155.

Watanabe, S. (1983), Technical cooperation between large and small firms in the Filipino automobile industry, in S. Watanabe (Ed.), *Technology, Marketing and Industrialisation: Linkages between Small and Large Enterprises*, Macmillan, New Delhi.

White, H. (1980), A heteroskedasticity-consistent covariance matrix estimator and a direct test for heteroskedasticity, *Econometrica*, **48**, 817–838.

Williamson, O. (1975), *Market and Hierarchies*, Free Press, New York.

Williamson, O. (1981), The modern corporation: origins, evolution, attributes, *Journal of Economic Literature*, **19**, 1537–1568.

Williamson, O. (1985), *The Economic Institutions of Capitalism*, Free Press, New York.

Young, S., Hood, N. and Hamill, J. (1988), *Foreign Multinationals and the British Economy: Impact and Policy*, Croom helm, London.

Zander, U. and Kogut, B. (1995), Knowledge and the speed of the transfer and imitation of organisational capabilities: an empirical test, *Organization Science*, **6**, 76–92.

# ˙Author Index

183

# Subject Index

185